Your Cup of Cake

Your Cup of Cake

by Lizzy Early

Printed in China
First Printing: March 2013
First Printing in Softcover: March 2017

23 22 21 20 19 18 17   10 9 8 7 6 5 4 3 2 1

ISBN-13: 978-1-52440-147-4

Lizzy Early grew up in Portland, Oregon, in a family of five. She started baking when she was in high school and quickly became known for her way around a kitchen. A 2013 graduate of Brigham Young University in broadcast journalism, she's the proud owner of www.YourCupofCake.com—and, more than anything, she loves to teach others how to bake.

This book is dedicated to

my parents,
Michael and Julie,

who washed a thousand dishes and lived in a kitchen dusted with powdered sugar for three months while I wrote this book. I love you both.

Table of Contents

Classic Cakes: 1

Thirsty for Cupcakes: 23

Sweet Breakfast: 45

Party Cakes: 61

All Dressed Up: 87

Stuffed and Filled: 111

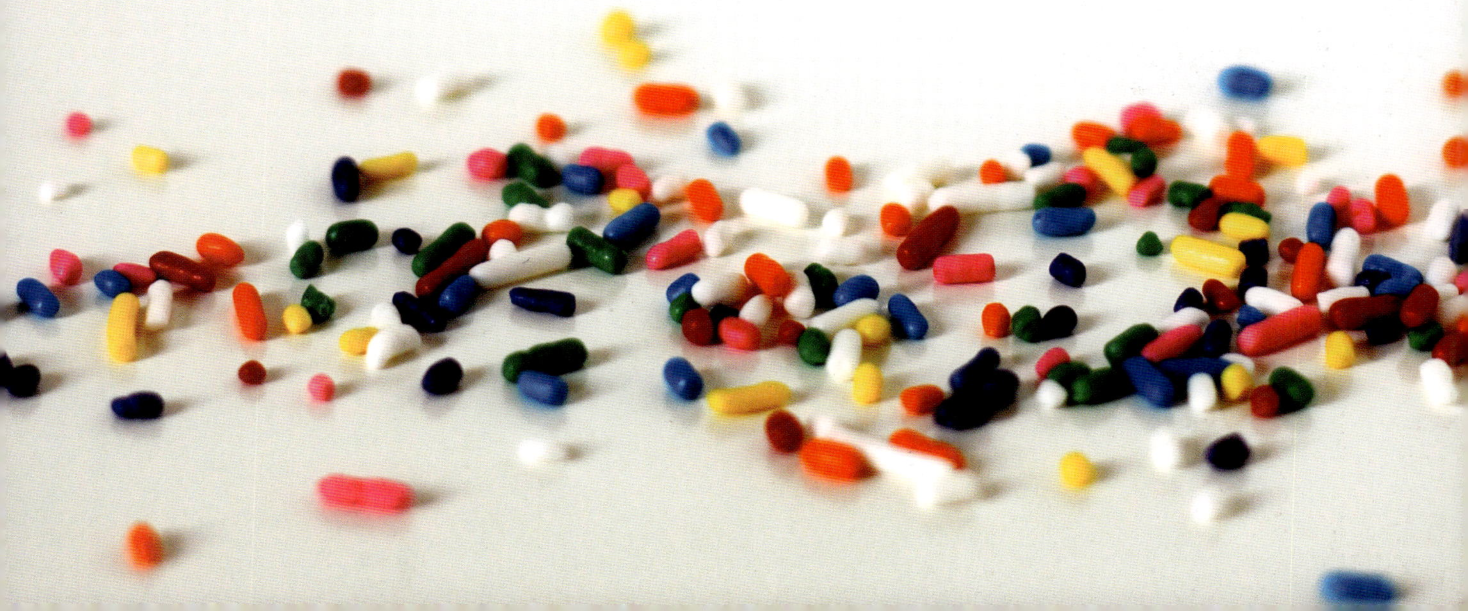

'Tis the Season for Cupcakes: 131

Cakes for Kids: 153

Tips and Tricks: 169

Index: 180

Classic Cakes

Yellow cake with chocolate frosting—that was the best cake in the world when I was six years old. Even though I've grown up a little and my taste buds have ventured to other flavors, biting into a yellow cupcake with silky smooth chocolate frosting is the ultimate dessert comfort food. Just one taste and I feel like I'm back on the playground.

Chocolate Vanilla Cupcakes

Vanilla Cupcakes:
1 box white cake mix
4 egg whites
⅓ C. oil
¾ C. buttermilk
¾ C. sour cream
2 tsp. vanilla extract

Chocolate Buttercream:
¾ C. butter, softened
4 oz. cream cheese, softened
¾ C. unsweetened cocoa powder
2 tsp. vanilla extract
3–4 C. powdered sugar
Milk, if needed
Sprinkles for garnish

Directions:

1. Preheat oven to 350 and line pans with cupcake liners.
2. Sift cake mix into a small bowl; set aside.
3. In a large bowl, gently whisk egg whites, oil, buttermilk, sour cream, and vanilla extract.
4. Add cake mix and stir until well combined.
5. Fill liners ¾ full and bake for 17–22 minutes or until a knife inserted in the center comes out clean.
6. For Chocolate Buttercream: Beat butter and cream cheese until light and fluffy. Add cocoa powder and vanilla extract. Slowly add powdered sugar until buttercream is the desired consistency. If it becomes too thick, add 1 T. milk.
7. Pipe buttercream onto cooled cupcakes and garnish with sprinkles.

Makes 24 cupcakes.

Double Chocolate Cupcakes

Chocolate Cupcakes:
1 box devil's food cake mix
3 eggs
½ C. oil
¾ C. buttermilk
1 C. sour cream
2 tsp. vanilla extract
1 tsp. cinnamon

Chocolate Buttercream:
½ C. butter, softened
8 oz. cream cheese
2 tsp. vanilla extract
¾ C. unsweetened cocoa powder
1 T. milk
3–4 C. powdered sugar

Directions:

1. Preheat oven to 350 and line pans with cupcake liners.
2. Sift cake mix into a bowl; set aside.
3. In a large bowl, gently whisk eggs, oil, buttermilk, sour cream, vanilla extract, and cinnamon.
4. Add cake mix and stir until well combined.
5. Fill cupcake liners ¾ full and bake for 16–22 minutes or until a knife inserted near the center comes out clean.
6. For Chocolate Buttercream: Beat butter and cream cheese for 2 minutes. Add vanilla extract, cocoa powder, and milk; beat again. Slowly add powdered sugar until buttercream is the desired consistency.
7. Pipe buttermilk on cooled cupcakes and top with sprinkles.

Makes 24 cupcakes.

Carrot Cupcakes with Cream Cheese Frosting

Carrot Cupcakes:
1 box yellow cake mix
3 tsp. cinnamon
½ tsp. ginger
½ tsp. nutmeg
3 eggs
⅓ C. oil
¾ C. buttermilk
⅓ C. sour cream
1 tsp. vanilla extract
½ C. crushed pineapple, well drained
2¾ C. grated carrots

Cream Cheese Frosting:
½ C. butter, softened
8 oz. cream cheese, softened
2 tsp. vanilla extract
3–5 C. powdered sugar
Chopped walnuts for garnish

Directions:

1. Preheat oven to 350 and line pans with cupcake liners.
2. Sift cake mix, cinnamon, ginger, and nutmeg into a small bowl; set aside.
3. In a large bowl, gently whisk eggs, oil, buttermilk, sour cream, vanilla extract, and pineapple.
4. Add cake mix mixture; stir well.
5. Add grated carrots; stir just until combined.
6. Fill cupcake liners ¾ full and bake for 18–25 minutes or until a knife inserted near the center comes out clean.
7. For Cream Cheese Frosting: Beat butter and cream cheese for 2 minutes. Add vanilla extract and slowly add powdered sugar until frosting is the desired consistency.
8. Pipe frosting onto cooled cupcakes and top with chopped walnuts.

Makes 28–32 cupcakes.

Very Vanilla Cupcakes

Vanilla Cupcakes:
1 box white cake mix
4 egg whites
⅓ C. oil
¾ C. buttermilk
½ C. mayonnaise
1 T. vanilla extract

Vanilla Bean Buttercream:
1 C. butter, softened
1 vanilla bean
3–4 C. powdered sugar
Milk, if needed
Sprinkles for garnish

Directions:

1. Preheat oven to 350 and line pans with cupcake liners.
2. Sift cake mix into a small bowl; set aside.
3. In a large bowl, gently whisk egg whites, oil, buttermilk, mayonnaise, and vanilla extract.
4. Stir in cake mix until well combined.
5. Fill cupcake liners ¾ full and bake for 17–22 minutes or until a knife inserted near the center comes out clean.
6. For Vanilla Bean Buttercream: Beat butter until light and fluffy. Split the vanilla bean lengthwise with a knife; use the tip of the knife to scrape out all of the beans. Add the beans to the butter. Slowly add powdered sugar until the buttercream is the desired consistency. If it becomes too thick, use a little milk to thin it.
7. Pipe buttercream onto cooled cupcakes and finish with sprinkles.

Makes 24 cupcakes.

Coconut Cream Cupcakes

Coconut Cupcakes:
1 box white cake mix
4 egg whites
⅓ C. oil
1 C. coconut milk
½ C. sour cream
1½ tsp. coconut extract
1½ tsp. vanilla extract

Coconut Cream:
½ C. butter, softened
8 oz. cream cheese, softened
1½ tsp. coconut extract
4–5 C. powdered sugar
Coconut flakes for decoration

Directions:

1. Preheat oven to 350 and line pans with cupcake liners.
2. Sift cake mix into a small bowl; set aside.
3. In a large bowl, gently whisk egg whites, oil, coconut milk, sour cream, coconut extract, and vanilla extract.
4. Add cake mix; stir until well combined.
5. Fill cupcake liners ¾ full and bake for 17–22 minutes or until a knife inserted near the center comes out clean.
6. For Coconut Cream: Beat butter and cream cheese for 2 minutes. Add coconut extract. Slowly add powdered sugar until coconut cream is the desired consistency.
7. Pipe onto cooled cupcakes and immediately roll in coconut flakes.

Makes 24 cupcakes.

Chocolate Mint Cupcakes (Andes Mint™)

Chocolate Cupcakes:
1 box devil's food cake mix
3 eggs
½ C. oil
1 C. buttermilk
¾ C. sour cream
2 tsp. vanilla extract

Peppermint Chocolate Ganache:
1 C. chocolate chips
1 tsp. peppermint extract
4 T. whipping cream

Peppermint Buttercream:
¾ C. butter, softened
4 oz. cream cheese, softened
2 tsp. peppermint extract
4–5 C. powdered sugar
Green food coloring, optional
Chocolate peppermint candies (Andes Mints™) for garnish

Directions:

1. Preheat oven to 350 and line pans with cupcake liners.
2. Sift cake mix into a bowl; set aside.
3. In a large bowl, gently whisk eggs, oil, buttermilk, sour cream, and vanilla extract.
4. Add cake mix and stir until well combined.
5. Fill cupcake liners ¾ full and bake for 17–22 minutes or until a knife inserted near the center comes out clean.
6. Let cupcakes cool completely.
7. For Ganache: Place chocolate chips and peppermint extract in a heatproof bowl; set aside. Gently heat whipping cream until small bubbles form around the edges. Pour cream over the chocolate chips and whisk until smooth. Dip the top of each cooled cupcake into the ganache; let the ganache set until it is firm to the touch.
8. For Peppermint Buttercream: Beat butter and cream cheese for 2 minutes. Add peppermint extract and slowly add powdered sugar until buttercream is the desired consistency. Add green food coloring if desired.
9. Pipe buttercream on top of ganache; drizzle any extra ganache over the top of the cupcakes. Finish with a chocolate peppermint candy (Andes Mint™).

Makes 24 cupcakes.

Yellow Cupcakes with Chocolate Buttercream

Yellow Cupcakes:
1 box yellow cake mix
3 eggs
⅓ C. oil
1 C. buttermilk
½ C. mayonnaise
1½ tsp. vanilla extract

Buttercream:
1 C. butter, softened
2 tsp. vanilla extract
¾ C. unsweetened cocoa
1 T. milk
3–4 C. powdered sugar
Chocolate sprinkles for garnish

Directions:

1. Preheat oven to 350 and line pans with cupcake liners.
2. Sift cake mix into a small bowl; set aside.
3. In a large bowl, gently whisk eggs, oil, buttermilk, mayonnaise, and vanilla extract.
4. Add cake mix and stir until well combined.
5. Fill cupcake liners ¾ full and bake for 17–22 minutes or until a knife inserted near the center comes out clean.
6. For Buttercream: Beat butter for 2 minutes. Add vanilla extract, cocoa, and milk. Slowly add powdered sugar until buttercream is the desired consistency.
7. Pipe onto cooled cupcakes and top with chocolate sprinkles.

Makes 24 cupcakes.

German Chocolate Cupcakes

Chocolate Cake:
1 box German chocolate cake mix
3 eggs
½ C. oil
¾ C. buttermilk
1 C. sour cream
1½ tsp. vanilla extract

German Chocolate Frosting:
1 C. evaporated milk
1 C. granulated sugar
3 egg yolks, lightly beaten
½ C. butter
1½ tsp. vanilla extract
1½ C. chopped pecans
1½ C. flaked coconut

Chocolate Buttercream:
4 oz. cream cheese
½ C. butter
2/3 C. unsweetened cocoa powder
3 C. powdered sugar
2 tsp. vanilla extract
Milk, if needed

Directions:

1. Preheat oven to 350 and line pans with cupcake liners.
2. Sift cake mix into a small bowl; set aside.
3. In a large bowl, gently whisk eggs, oil, buttermilk, sour cream, and vanilla extract.
4. Add cake mix and stir until well combined.
5. Fill cupcake liners ¾ full and bake for 17–22 minutes or until a knife inserted near the center comes out clean.
6. For German Chocolate Frosting: In a medium saucepan over medium heat, constantly stir evaporated milk, sugar, egg yolks, and butter until thick, about 10–15 minutes. Stir in vanilla extract, pecans, and coconut. Let cool.
7. For Chocolate Buttercream: Beat cream cheese and butter for 2 minutes. Add cocoa, powdered sugar, and vanilla extract. Add 1 T. milk if the buttercream becomes too thick.
8. To assemble, pipe a decorative circle of chocolate buttercream around the edge of the cupcake, then place a small mound of German chocolate frosting in the center.

Makes 24 cupcakes.

Peanut Butter and Chocolate Cupcakes

Chocolate Cupcakes:
1 box devil's food cake mix
3 eggs
½ C. oil
1 C. buttermilk
¾ C. sour cream
2 tsp. vanilla extract

Peanut Butter Chocolate Topping:
⅔ C. chocolate chips
⅓ C. smooth peanut butter

Peanut Butter Frosting:
½ C. butter, softened
½ C. smooth peanut butter
2 T. milk
2 tsp. vanilla extract
3–4 C. powdered sugar
Sprinkles for garnish
Chocolate peanut butter cups for decoration

Directions:

1. Preheat oven to 350 and line pans with cupcake liners.
2. Sift cake mix into a small bowl; set aside.
3. In a large bowl, gently whisk eggs, oil, buttermilk, sour cream, and vanilla extract.
4. Add cake mix and stir until well combined.
5. Fill cupcake liners ¾ full and bake for 17–22 minutes or until a knife inserted near the center comes out clean. Let cool completely.
6. For Peanut Butter Chocolate Topping: In a small saucepan over medium heat, melt chocolate chips and peanut butter. Stir until smooth. Dip the top of each cooled cupcake into the topping and let set until firm.
7. For Peanut Butter Frosting: Beat butter and peanut butter for 2 minutes. Add milk and vanilla extract. Slowly add powdered sugar until frosting is the desired consistency.
8. Pipe frosting over cooled ganache and top with sprinkles and chocolate peanut butter cups.

Makes 24 cupcakes.

Banana Cream Cupcakes with Chocolate Ganache

Banana Cupcakes:
1 box yellow cake mix
1/3 C. flour
3 ripe bananas, medium size
1 tsp. baking soda
½ tsp. lemon juice
3 eggs
⅓ C. oil
¾ C. buttermilk
¾ C. sour cream
1 T. vanilla extract

Cream Cheese Frosting:
½ C. butter, softened
8 oz. cream cheese, softened
2 tsp. vanilla extract
¾ C. powdered sugar

Chocolate Ganache:
½ C. chocolate chips
⅓ C. whipping cream
1½ T. honey
Sliced banana for decoration

Directions:

1. Preheat oven to 350 and line pans with cupcake liners.
2. Sift cake mix and flour into a small bowl; set aside.
3. In another bowl, use a fork to finely mash bananas with baking soda and lemon juice. Set aside.
4. In a large bowl, gently whisk eggs, oil, buttermilk, sour cream, and vanilla extract.
5. Add mashed bananas and cake mix to the egg mixture; stir until well combined.
6. Fill cupcake liners ¾ full and bake for 17–22 minutes or until a knife inserted near the center comes out clean.
7. For Cream Cheese Frosting: Beat butter and cream cheese for 2 minutes. Add vanilla extract and slowly add powdered sugar until frosting is the desired consistency.
8. For Chocolate Ganache: Place chocolate chips in a heatproof bowl; set aside. Over the stove, heat whipping cream until small bubbles form around the edges. Pour hot cream over chocolate chips and whisk until smooth. Add honey and stir.
9. To assemble, pipe cream cheese frosting over cooled cupcakes, spoon ganache on top, and finish with a slice of banana.

Makes 28 cupcakes.

Thirsty for Cupcakes

I'm an American girl—I love fries, hot dogs, burgers, fried chicken, and milkshakes. When I was little, I always ordered a chocolate malt. Did I know what malt was? No. Did any of my friends order a malt? No. But my father always did. So I always did.

Chocolate Malt Cupcakes

Chocolate Malt Cupcakes:
1 box devil's food cake mix
½ C. malted milk powder
3 eggs
½ C. oil
¾ C. buttermilk
¾ C. sour cream
2 tsp. vanilla extract

Chocolate Malt Buttercream:
¾ C. butter, softened
4 oz. cream cheese, softened
¾ C. unsweetened cocoa powder
2 tsp. vanilla extract
2–4 C. powdered sugar
½ C. malted milk powder
1 T. milk, if needed
Straws for decoration
Chocolate-covered malt balls for decoration

Directions:

1. Preheat oven to 350 and line pans with cupcake liners.
2. Sift cake mix and malted milk powder into a small bowl; set aside.
3. In a large bowl, combine eggs, oil, buttermilk, sour cream, and vanilla extract until smooth.
4. Add sifted cake mix and malted milk powder; stir until combined well.
5. Fill cupcake liners ¾ full and bake for 17–22 minutes or until a knife inserted near the center comes out clean.
6. For Chocolate Malt Buttercream: Beat butter and cream cheese for 2 minutes. Add cocoa powder and vanilla extract; beat again, scraping down bowl as needed. Slowly add powdered sugar and malted milk powder until buttercream reaches desired consistency. If it becomes too thick, add 1 T. milk.
7. Pipe buttercream onto cooled cupcakes; top with a straw and a chocolate-covered malt ball.

Makes 24 cupcakes.

Pink Lemonade Cupcakes

Lemon Cupcakes:
1 box white or lemon cake mix
4 egg whites
⅓ C. oil
¾ C. milk
⅓ C. plain yogurt
¼ C. lemon juice
2 T. lemon zest

Strawberry Buttercream:
1 C. butter, softened
1 tsp. vanilla extract
4–5 C. powdered sugar
2–4 T. strawberry puree
Straws for decoration

Directions:

1. Preheat oven to 350 and line pans with cupcake liners.
2. Sift cake mix into a small bowl; set aside.
3. In a large bowl, combine egg whites, oil, milk, yogurt, lemon juice, and lemon zest until smooth.
4. Add cake mix; stir to combine well.
5. Fill cupcake liners ¾ full and bake for 17–22 minutes or until a knife inserted near the center comes out clean.
6. For Strawberry Buttercream: Beat butter for 2 minutes. Add vanilla extract. Slowly add powdered sugar until buttercream is a consistency slightly thicker than desired. Slowly stir in strawberry puree (fresh strawberries that have been processed in a blender to soup-like consistency). Add only as much puree as needed to make buttercream the right consistency. If the buttercream becomes too thin, add more powdered sugar.
7. Pipe buttercream onto cooled cupcakes and decorate with straws.

Makes 24 cupcakes.

©Wilton

Lemon-Lime Cupcakes

Lemon-Lime Cupcakes:
1 box white cake mix
4 egg whites
⅓ C. oil
½ C. buttermilk
¼ C. lemon-lime soda
½ C. sour cream
2 T. lime juice
1½ T. lime zest

Lemon Buttercream:
½ C. butter, softened
8 oz. cream cheese, softened
2 T. lemon zest
1 T. lemon juice
4–5 C. powdered sugar
Sprinkles or lemon zest for garnish

Directions:

1. Preheat oven to 350 and line pans with cupcake liners.
2. Sift cake mix into a small bowl; set aside.
3. In a large bowl, use a whisk to combine egg whites, oil, buttermilk, soda, sour cream, lime juice, and lime zest until smooth.
4. Add cake mix and stir until combined well.
5. Fill cupcake liners ¾ full and bake for 17–22 minute or until a knife inserted near the center comes out clean.
6. For Lemon Buttercream: Beat butter and cream cheese for 2 minutes. Add lemon zest and lemon juice; beat again. Scrape down the sides of the bowl as needed. Slowly add powdered sugar until buttercream is the desired consistency. If the buttercream becomes too thick, add more lemon juice.
7. Pipe buttercream onto cooled cupcakes and top with sprinkles or extra lemon zest.

Makes 24 cupcakes.

Mint Limeade Cupcakes

Limeade Cupcakes:
1 box white cake mix
4 egg whites
⅓ C. oil
½ C. milk
¼ C. lime juice
½ C. plain yogurt or sour cream
2 T. lime zest

Mint Lime Buttercream:
1 C. butter, softened
2½ tsp. lime zest
2 tsp. chopped mint leaves
4–5 C. powdered sugar
1 T. milk, if needed
Mint leaves for decoration
Lime slices for decoration

Directions:

1. Preheat oven to 350 and line pans with cupcake liners.
2. Sift cake mix into a small bowl; set aside.
3. In a large bowl, combine egg whites, oil, milk, lime juice, yogurt, and lime zest.
4. Add cake mix and stir until smooth.
5. Fill cupcake liners ¾ full and bake for 17–22 minutes or until a knife inserted near the center comes out clean.
6. For Mint Lime Buttercream: Beat butter for 2 minutes. Add lime zest and mint leaves. Slowly add powdered sugar until buttercream reaches desired consistency. If it becomes too thick, add milk.
7. Pipe buttercream onto cooled cupcakes; decorate with mint leaves and lime slices.

Makes 24 cupcakes.

Apple Cider Cupcakes

Apple Cupcakes:
1 box white or yellow cake mix
2 tsp. cinnamon
3 eggs
¼ C. oil
½ C. applesauce
½ C. milk
1½ tsp. orange zest
2 tsp. vanilla extract

Spiced Cider Buttercream:
1 C. butter, softened
1 tsp. vanilla extract
4–5 C. powdered sugar
1 T. milk, if needed
2–3 tsp. instant spiced apple cider mix
Cinnamon sugar for garnish
Cinnamon sticks for garnish

Directions:

1. Preheat oven to 350 and line pans with cupcake liners.
2. Sift cake mix and cinnamon into a small bowl; set aside.
3. In a large bowl, combine eggs, oil, applesauce, milk, orange zest, and vanilla extract.
4. Stir in sifted cake mix and cinnamon until smooth.
5. Fill cupcake liners ¾ full and bake for 17–22 minutes or until a knife inserted near the center comes out clean.
6. For Spiced Cider Buttercream: Beat butter for 2 minutes. Add vanilla extract. Slowly add powdered sugar until buttercream reaches desired consistency. Add milk if it becomes too thick. Add cider mix a little at a time until you reach the taste you want; make sure you taste with each addition, since the mix is surprisingly strong.
7. Pipe buttercream onto cooled cupcakes; top with cinnamon sugar and cinnamon sticks.

Makes 24 cupcakes.

Mexican Hot Chocolate Cupcakes

Chocolate Cupcakes:
- 1 box devil's food cake mix
- 1 3.4-oz. pkg. instant chocolate pudding mix
- 3 tsp. cinnamon
- 4 eggs
- 2/3 C. oil
- ¾ C. milk
- ½ C. sour cream
- 2 tsp. vanilla extract

Cinnamon Whipped Cream Topping:
- 8 oz. cream cheese, softened
- 1 C. powdered sugar
- 1 tsp. vanilla extract
- 1 tsp. cinnamon
- 1 pint heavy whipping cream
- Marshmallows tossed in cinnamon for decoration

Directions:
1. Preheat oven to 350 and line pans with cupcake liners.
2. Sift cake mix, instant pudding mix, and cinnamon into a small bowl; set aside.
3. In a large bowl, combine eggs, oil, milk, sour cream, and vanilla extract until smooth.
4. Add sifted cake mix mixture and stir until combined well.
5. Fill cupcake liners ¾ full and bake for 17–22 minutes or until a knife inserted near the center comes out clean.
6. For Cinnamon Whipped Cream Topping: Using the paddle attachment on a stand mixer, combine cream cheese, powdered sugar, vanilla extract, and cinnamon until smooth. Switch to the whisk attachment; with the mixer on medium-high, slowly pour in heavy whipping cream. Beat until stiff peaks form.
7. Pipe onto cooled cupcakes and top with marshmallows that have been coated with cinnamon.

Makes 24 cupcakes.

Orange Cream Soda Cupcakes

Orange Cream Cupcakes:
1 box white cake mix
1 3.4-oz. pkg. cheesecake or vanilla instant pudding mix
4 eggs
2/3 C. oil
½ C. milk
¼ C. orange juice
½ C. sour cream
2 T. orange zest

Orange Cream Buttercream:
½ C. butter, softened
8 oz. cream cheese, softened
2 tsp. orange-flavored gelatin
2 tsp. orange zest
1 tsp. vanilla extract
4–5 C. powdered sugar
1 T. milk, if needed
Sprinkles for decoration

Directions:

1. Preheat oven to 350 and line pans with cupcake liners.
2. Sift cake mix and instant pudding mix into a small bowl; set aside.
3. In a large bowl, combine eggs, oil, milk, orange juice, sour cream, and orange zest until smooth.
4. Add sifted cake mix mixture; stir until combined well.
5. Fill cupcake liners ¾ full and bake for 17–22 minutes or until a knife inserted near the center comes out clean.
6. For Orange Cream Buttercream: Beat butter and cream cheese for 2 minutes. Add gelatin, orange zest, and vanilla extract; beat again. Slowly add powdered sugar until buttercream reaches desired consistency. If it becomes too thick, add 1 T. milk.
7. Pipe onto cooled cupcakes and decorate with sprinkles.

Makes 24 cupcakes.

Cranberry Eggnog Cupcakes

Cranberry Eggnog Cupcakes:
1 box white or yellow cake mix
1 tsp. nutmeg
3 eggs
6 T. butter, melted and cooled
¾ C. eggnog
½ C. sour cream
1 tsp. vanilla extract
1 C. fresh or dried cranberries (if you use fresh, coarsely chop them)

Eggnog Buttercream:
1 C. butter, softened
½ tsp. nutmeg
½ tsp. instant apple cider mix
4–5 C. powdered sugar
2–4 T. eggnog
Sprinkles for garnish

Directions:

1. Preheat oven to 350 and line pans with cupcake liners.
2. Sift cake mix and nutmeg into a small bowl; set aside.
3. In a large bowl, combine eggs, butter, eggnog, sour cream, and vanilla extract until smooth.
4. Add sifted cake mix mixture; stir until well combined.
5. Add cranberries and stir.
6. Fill cupcake liners ¾ full and bake for 17–22 minutes or until a knife inserted near the center comes out clean.
7. For Eggnog Buttercream: Beat butter for 2 minutes. Add nutmeg and instant apple cider mix. Slowly add powdered sugar until buttercream reaches a consistency slightly thicker than desired. Stir in eggnog until buttercream is the desired consistency. If it becomes too thin, add more powdered sugar.
8. Pipe onto cooled cupcakes and top with sprinkles.

Makes 24 cupcakes.

Shirley Temple Cupcakes

Cupcakes:
1 box white cake mix
4 egg whites
⅓ C. oil
½ C. milk
¼ C. lemon-lime soda
½ C. sour cream
3 tsp. vanilla extract
1 tsp. almond extract
1 T. maraschino cherry juice
2 tsp. flour
Red food dye, optional

Vanilla Buttercream:
1 C. butter, softened
2 tsp. vanilla extract
½ tsp. almond extract
1 T. maraschino cherry juice
4–5 C. powdered sugar
Maraschino cherries for decoration

Directions:

1. Preheat oven to 350 and line pans with cupcake liners.
2. Sift cake mix into a small bowl; set aside.
3. In a large bowl, combine egg whites, oil, milk, soda, sour cream, vanilla extract, and almond extract until smooth.
4. Stir in cake mix; combine well.
5. Remove a heaping ½ C. batter and place in a small bowl. Stir in maraschino cherry juice and flour until smooth. Add red food dye if desired.
6. Place 1–2 tsp. of red batter in the bottom of each cupcake liner; cover with white batter until liners are ¾ full. Bake for 17–22 minutes or until a knife inserted near the center comes out clean.
7. For Vanilla Buttercream: Beat butter for 2 minutes; add vanilla extract, almond extract, and maraschino cherry juice. Slowly add powdered sugar until buttercream reaches desired consistency.
8. Pipe onto cooled cupcakes and top with maraschino cherries.

Makes 24 cupcakes.

Root Beer Float Cupcakes

Root Beer Cupcakes:
1 box white cake mix
3 eggs
⅓ C. oil
¼ C. milk
½ C. root beer
¾ C. sour cream
2 tsp. root beer concentrate

Vanilla Bean Buttercream:
½ C. butter, softened
8 oz. cream cheese, softened
1 vanilla bean (or 1 T. vanilla extract)
4–5 C. powdered sugar
1 T. milk, if needed
Straws for decoration

Directions:

1. Preheat oven to 350 and line pans with cupcake liners.
2. Sift cake mix into a small bowl; set aside.
3. In a large bowl, combine eggs, oil, milk, root beer, sour cream, and root beer concentrate until smooth.
4. Add sifted cake mix; stir until well combined.
5. Fill cupcake liners ¾ full and bake for 17–22 minutes or until a knife inserted near the center comes out clean.
6. For Vanilla Bean Buttercream: Beat butter and cream cheese for 2 minutes. Using a knife, split vanilla bean lengthwise; using the tip of the knife, scrape out all the beans. Add the beans to the butter/cream cheese mixture and discard the pod. Slowly add powdered sugar until buttercream reaches desired consistency. If it gets too thick, add milk.
7. Pipe buttercream onto cooled cupcakes and top with straws.

Makes 24 cupcakes.

Sweet Breakfast

There's a reason you'll never see a restaurant advertise, "We serve dinner food all day long." It's all about breakfast food. Pancakes, waffles, orange juice, even crepes always sound good, even if it's midnight and cricket songs fill the air.

Blueberry Pancake Cupcakes

Blueberry Cupcakes:
1 box white cake mix
1 tsp. cinnamon
3 eggs
⅓ C. oil
¾ C. buttermilk
¾ C. sour cream
2 tsp. vanilla extract
1½ C. blueberries (fresh or frozen)

Maple Buttercream:
1 C. butter, softened
1 T. milk
4–5 C. powdered sugar
1–2 tsp. maple flavoring
Blueberries for garnish
Cinnamon sugar for garnish

Directions:

1. Preheat oven to 350 and line pans with cupcake liners.
2. Sift cake mix and cinnamon into a small bowl; set aside.
3. In a large bowl, combine eggs, oil, buttermilk, sour cream, and vanilla extract.
4. Stir in cake mix and cinnamon until smooth.
5. Fold in blueberries.
6. Fill cupcake liners ¾ full and bake for 17–23 minutes or until a knife inserted near the center comes out clean. (If you use frozen blueberries, it may take a little longer.)
7. For Maple Buttercream: Beat butter for 2 minutes. Scrape down the bowl and stir in milk. Slowly add powdered sugar until buttercream is the desired consistency. Add maple flavoring; adjust for flavor depending on the brand of flavoring you use.
8. Pipe buttercream onto cooled cupcakes; top with blueberries and cinnamon sugar.

Makes 24 cupcakes.

Cinnamon Toast Crunch Cupcakes

Cinnamon Cupcakes:
1 box white cake mix
2 tsp. cinnamon
3 eggs
⅓ C. oil
¾ C. buttermilk
¾ C. sour cream
2 tsp. vanilla extract

Cinnamon Toast Crunch Buttercream:
2/3 C. Cinnamon Toast Crunch Cereal
½ C. butter, softened
8 oz. cream cheese, softened
1 tsp. vanilla extract
3–4 C. powdered sugar
1 T. milk, if needed
Cinnamon sugar for garnish
Cinnamon Toast Crunch Cereal for garnish

Directions:

1. Preheat oven to 350 and line pans with cupcake liners.
2. Sift cake mix and cinnamon into a small bowl; set aside.
3. In a large bowl, combine eggs, oil, buttermilk, sour cream, and vanilla extract.
4. Add cake mix and cinnamon and stir until smooth.
5. Fill cupcake liners ¾ full and bake for 17–22 minutes or until a knife inserted near the center comes out clean.
6. For Cinnamon Toast Crunch Buttercream: Using a food processor, finely crush Cinnamon Toast Crunch cereal. Sift out the large pieces; you should use only the "powder" that goes through the sifter. Set aside. In a stand mixer, beat butter and cream cheese for 2 minutes. Add vanilla extract and cereal "powder." Slowly add powdered sugar until buttercream is the desired consistency. If the buttercream is too thick, add 1 T. milk (or more) to achieve a creamy consistency.
7. Pipe buttercream onto cooled cupcakes; top with cinnamon sugar and Cinnamon Toast Crunch cereal pieces.

Makes 24 cupcakes.

Fruity Cereal Cupcakes

Pineapple Cupcakes:
1 box white or yellow cake mix
3 eggs
½ C. oil
½ C. milk
¼ C. pineapple juice
½ C. crushed pineapple, drained

Cereal Buttercream:
⅓ C. red and orange cereal pieces
⅓ C. blue and green cereal pieces
⅓ C. purple cereal pieces
1½ C. butter, softened
5–6 C. powdered sugar
3 T. milk, if needed
1 tsp. orange-flavored gelatin, optional
1 tsp. blue raspberry-flavored gelatin, optional
1 tsp. grape-flavored gelatin, optional
Cereal pieces for garnish

Directions:

1. Preheat oven to 350 and line pans with cupcake liners.
2. Sift cake mix into a small bowl; set aside.
3. In a large bowl, combine eggs, oil, milk, pineapple juice, and pineapple. Make sure to drain the crushed pineapple as thoroughly as possible; too much juice will make the batter too thin.
4. Stir in cake mix until smooth.
5. Fill cupcake liners ¾ full and bake for 17–22 minutes or until a knife inserted near the center comes out clean.
6. For Cereal Buttercream: Using a food processor, crush each group of cereal pieces separately; crush them as finely as possible. Using a stand mixer, beat butter until smooth; slowly add powdered sugar until the buttercream is slightly thinner than desired. Separate buttercream into 3 bowls; add one color of crushed cereal to each bowl. Mix in thoroughly; use milk to thin the buttercream if needed. For additional color and flavor, add the appropriate gelatin to each bowl if desired.
7. Pipe onto cooled cupcakes and top with cereal pieces.

Makes 24 cupcakes.

Cinnamon Rolls

Rolls:
3 .25-oz. pkgs. dry yeast
1 C. warm water
1½ C. warm milk
1 box white or yellow cake mix
1 tsp. salt
4½ C. flour
2 tsp. vanilla extract

Filling:
¾ C. butter, softened
2 C. brown sugar
3 tsp. cinnamon

Glaze:
1⅓ C. powdered sugar, sifted
3–4 T. milk or hot water

Directions:

1. Mix yeast with warm water and warm milk until dissolved.
2. In a separate bowl, sift cake mix, salt, and flour.
3. Add the yeast mixture and vanilla extract to the dry ingredients; knead by hand until evenly combined.
4. Cover with cloth and let rise in a warm place for 1 hour. Punch down then let rise for 30 more minutes.
5. Preheat oven to 350 and line pans with cupcake liners.
6. On a floured surface, roll dough into a large, long rectangle about ¼ inch thick.
7. For Filling: Spread butter over the dough; spread brown sugar over the butter and sprinkle cinnamon over the brown sugar.
8. Starting with the long side, roll the dough tightly into a long, skinny roll.
9. Using a sharp knife, cut the dough into 1½- or 2-inch pieces.
10. Place each roll in a cupcake liner; bake for 14–20 minutes or until the tops are firm to the touch and no longer doughy.
11. For Glaze: Using a fork or whisk, combine powdered sugar and milk or water. Spoon glaze over warm cinnamon rolls.

Makes 40 cinnamon rolls.

ON THE ERIE CANAL
Spencerport, Pittsford,

Oatmeal Raisin Cupcakes

Cinnamon Raisin Cupcakes:
1 box white cake mix
3 tsp. cinnamon
3 eggs
⅓ C. butter, melted and cooled
¾ C. milk
½ C. plain yogurt
2 tsp. vanilla extract
1 C. raisins

Oatmeal Buttercream:
¼ C. instant oatmeal
1 C. butter, softened
2 tsp. vanilla extract
3–4 C. powdered sugar
1 T. milk, if needed
Cinnamon sugar for garnish

Directions:

1. Preheat oven to 350 and line pans with cupcake liners.
2. Sift cake mix and cinnamon into a small bowl; set aside.
3. In a large bowl, combine eggs, butter, milk, yogurt, and vanilla extract.
4. Stir in cake mix and cinnamon until smooth.
5. Stir in raisins.
6. Fill cupcake liners ¾ full and bake for 17–22 minutes or until a knife inserted near the center comes out clean.
7. For Oatmeal Buttercream: Use a blender or food processor to finely chop the oatmeal. Set aside. In a stand mixer, beat butter for 2 minutes. Add vanilla extract and oatmeal. Slowly add powdered sugar until buttercream reaches desired consistency. If the buttercream is thick like cookie dough, add milk to achieve a creamy consistency.
8. Pipe onto cooled cupcakes and top with cinnamon sugar.

Makes 24 cupcakes.

French Toast Cupcakes

Cupcakes:
1 box white or yellow cake mix
1 tsp. nutmeg
1 tsp. cinnamon
3 eggs + 1 egg yolk
⅓ C. butter, melted and cooled
1 C. milk
¼ C. sour cream
1 T. vanilla extract

Egg Wash:
1 egg
2 tsp. milk

Maple Buttercream:
1 C. butter, softened
1 T. milk
4–5 C. powdered sugar
1–2 tsp. maple flavoring
Fresh fruit for garnish
Powdered sugar for garnish

Directions:

1. Preheat oven to 350 and line pans with cupcake liners.
2. Sift cake mix, nutmeg, and cinnamon into a bowl; set aside.
3. In a large bowl, combine eggs, ⅓ C. butter, 1 C. milk, sour cream, and vanilla extract.
4. Add sifted cake mix mixture and stir until smooth.
5. Fill cupcake liners ¾ full and bake for 16–20 minutes or just until they are 1 minute away from being done; brush on egg wash.
6. For Egg Wash: Using a fork or whisk, combine egg and 2 tsp. milk. Brush mixture onto the tops of nearly-done cupcakes; broil for 1–2 minutes until the tops of the cupcakes are golden brown and look like French toast. Watch the cupcakes closely because they can burn easily.
7. For Maple Buttercream: Beat 1 C. butter for 2 minutes. Scrape down the bowl and stir in milk. Slowly add powdered sugar until buttercream is the desired consistency. Add maple flavoring; adjust for flavor depending on the brand of flavoring you use.
8. Pipe buttercream onto cooled cupcakes; top with fresh fruit and powdered sugar.

Makes 24 cupcakes.

Maple Bacon Cupcakes

Vanilla Nutmeg Cupcakes:
1 box white cake mix
1½ tsp. nutmeg
3 eggs
⅓ C. oil
¾ C. milk
¾ C. sour cream
1 T. vanilla extract

Maple Buttercream:
1 C. butter, softened
1 T. milk
4–5 C. powdered sugar
1–2 tsp. maple flavoring
8–10 slices cooked bacon for garnish

Directions:

1. Preheat oven to 350 and line pans with cupcake liners.
2. Sift cake mix and nutmeg into a bowl; set aside.
3. In a large bowl, combine eggs, oil, milk, sour cream, and vanilla extract.
4. Add cake mix and nutmeg mixture; stir until smooth.
5. Fill cupcake liners ¾ full and bake for 17–22 minutes or until a knife inserted near the center comes out clean.
6. For Maple Buttercream: Beat butter for 2 minutes. Scrape down the bowl and stir in 1 T. milk. Slowly add powdered sugar until buttercream is the desired consistency. Add maple flavoring; adjust for flavor depending on the brand of flavoring you use.
7. Pipe onto cooled cupcakes; top with crumbled bacon to give cupcakes a salty and crunchy taste.

Makes 24 cupcakes.

Party Cakes

When I go to my parents' home to bake, I usually get a little frantic because I can't seem to find anything I need. But in those moments of frustration I rummage through the drawer that holds the little star cake pans, and my panic melts away as sweet memories fill my head. The cake was covered in white and pink frosting and had baby star cakes all around the sides. My mother must have slaved over it to have it ready in time for my gymnastics party. Birthday party cakes are the ones we never forget.

Banana Split Cupcakes

Cupcakes:
1 box white or yellow cake mix
3 eggs
⅓ C. oil
½ C. milk
½ C. sour cream
2 tsp. vanilla extract
¾ C. mashed bananas

Strawberry Buttercream:
¼ C. butter, softened
4 oz. cream cheese, softened
1 tsp. vanilla extract
2–3 C. powdered sugar
1–2 T. strawberry puree
1 tsp. strawberry-flavored gelatin, optional

Vanilla Cream Buttercream:
¼ C. butter, softened
4 oz. cream cheese, softened
1 tsp. vanilla extract
1 T. whipping cream
2–3 C. powdered sugar
Melted chocolate, sprinkles, and cherries for decoration

Directions:
1. Preheat oven to 350 and line pans with cupcake liners.
2. Sift cake mix into a small bowl; set aside.
3. In a large bowl, combine eggs, oil, milk, sour cream, and vanilla extract.
4. Stir in sifted cake mix and mashed bananas until mixture is smooth.
5. Fill cupcake liners ¾ full and bake for 17–22 minutes or until a knife inserted near the center comes out clean. Cool completely.
6. For Strawberry Buttercream: Beat butter and cream cheese for 2 minutes; add vanilla extract. Slowly add powdered sugar until the buttercream becomes a little thicker than desired. Slowly stir in strawberry puree (fresh strawberries pureed in a blender) until buttercream reaches desired consistency. For extra flavor and color, add strawberry-flavored gelatin.
7. For Vanilla Cream Buttercream: Beat butter and cream cheese for 2 minutes. Stir in vanilla extract and whipping cream. Slowly add powdered sugar until buttercream reaches desired consistency.
8. Fill a piping bag carefully with Strawberry Buttercream along one side and Vanilla Cream Buttercream along the other side. Pipe onto cooled cupcakes.
9. Top with melted chocolate, sprinkles, and cherries.

Makes 24 cupcakes.

Strawberry Vanilla Cupcakes

Vanilla Cupcakes:
1 box white cake mix
4 egg whites
⅓ C. oil
1 C. milk
¼ C. mayonnaise
1 T. vanilla extract

Strawberry Buttercream:
1 C. butter, softened
1 tsp. vanilla extract
4–5 C. powdered sugar
2–4 T. strawberry puree (see note)
Fresh strawberries or sprinkles for decoration

Directions:

1. Preheat oven to 350 degrees and line pans with cupcake liners.
2. Sift cake mix into a small bowl; set aside.
3. In a large bowl, use a whisk to gently combine egg whites, oil, milk, mayonnaise, and vanilla extract until smooth.
4. Add sifted cake mix and stir until combined well.
5. Fill cupcake liners ¾ full and bake for 17–22 minutes or until a knife inserted near the center comes out clean. Let cool completely.
6. For Strawberry Buttercream: Beat butter for 2 minutes, constantly scraping down the sides of the bowl. Add vanilla extract; stir. Slowly add powdered sugar until buttercream reaches a thick consistency. Slowly add strawberry puree until buttercream is the desired consistency (you might not need all of the puree). If the buttercream becomes too thin, add more powdered sugar.
7. Pipe buttercream onto cooled cupcakes and top with sprinkles or a fresh strawberry.

Note: Make strawberry puree by using a blender to process fresh strawberries until they are a soup-like consistency. Because the seeds are soft, strawberry puree does not have to be strained.

Makes 20–24 cupcakes.

Butterscotch Cupcakes

Vanilla Cupcakes:
1 box white cake mix
3 eggs
⅓ C. oil
1 C. milk
2 tsp. vanilla extract

Butterscotch Buttercream:
⅓ C. butterscotch chips
1 C. butter, softened
1 tsp. vanilla extract
4–5 C. powdered sugar

Butterscotch Coating:
2 C. butterscotch chips
3 T. oil

Directions:

1. Preheat oven to 350 and line pans with cupcake liners.
2. Sift cake mix into a small bowl; set aside.
3. In a large bowl, combine eggs, oil, milk, and vanilla extract.
4. Add sifted cake mix and stir until smooth.
5. Fill cupcake liners ¾ full and bake for 17–22 minutes or until a knife inserted near the center comes out clean. Cool completely.
6. For Butterscotch Buttercream: Using a food processor, pulverize ⅓ C. butterscotch chips. Set aside. In a stand mixer, beat butter for 2 minutes and add vanilla extract. Slowly add powdered sugar until buttercream reaches desired consistency. Add pulverized butterscotch chips and mix until evenly incorporated.
7. Pipe buttercream onto cooled cupcakes.
8. For Butterscotch Coating: Combine 2 C. butterscotch chips and oil; melt in the microwave or on the stove top, stirring frequently to keep from burning. Place Butterscotch Coating in a tall container. Submerge frosted cupcake into the Butterscotch Coating and immediately pull out; let cool.

Makes 20–24 cupcakes.

Confetti Cupcakes

Confetti Cupcakes:
1 box white cake mix
4 egg whites
⅓ C. oil
1 C. milk
⅓ C. mayonnaise
2 tsp. vanilla extract
½ tsp. almond extract
¼ C. multicolored sprinkles

Vanilla Buttercream:
1 C. butter
3 tsp. vanilla extract
4–5 C. powdered sugar
1 T. milk, if needed
Multicolored sprinkles for garnish

Directions:

1. Preheat oven to 350 and line pans with cupcake liners.
2. Sift cake mix into a small bowl; set aside.
3. In a large bowl, use a whisk to gently combine egg whites, oil, milk, mayonnaise, vanilla extract, and almond extract.
4. Add cake mix; stir until well combined.
5. Gently fold in ¼ C. multicolored sprinkles.
6. Fill cupcake liners ¾ full and bake for 17–22 minutes or until a knife inserted near the center comes out clean. Let cool completely.
7. For Vanilla Buttercream: Beat butter for 2 minutes. Scrape down the sides of the bowl and beat again. Add vanilla extract; slowly add powdered sugar until buttercream reaches desired consistency. If the buttercream becomes too thick, add 1 T. milk.
8. Pipe buttercream onto cooled cupcakes and top with multicolored sprinkles.

Makes 20–24 cupcakes.

Peaches and Cream Cupcakes

Peach Cupcakes:
1 box white cake mix
2 tsp. cinnamon
3 eggs
⅓ C. melted butter, cooled
¾ C. + 1 T. buttermilk
¼ C. peaches, peeled, pitted, and pureed
2 tsp. vanilla extract
1¼ C. peaches, chopped

Cream Cheese Buttercream:
8 oz. cream cheese, softened
½ C. butter, softened
2 tsp. vanilla extract
4–5 C. powdered sugar
Fresh peach slices for decoration

Directions:

1. Preheat oven to 350 and line pans with cupcake liners.
2. Sift cake mix and cinnamon into a small bowl; set aside.
3. In a large bowl, combine eggs, melted butter, buttermilk, peach puree, and vanilla extract until smooth.
4. Add cake mix and cinnamon; stir until smooth.
5. Fold in chopped peaches.
6. Fill cupcake liners ¾ full and bake for 17–23 minutes or until a knife inserted near the center comes out clean. Cupcakes with pieces of fresh fruit in them sometimes take a little longer to bake, so be patient. Let cool completely.
7. For Cream Cheese Buttercream: Beat butter and cream cheese for 2 minutes. Scrape down the sides of the bowl and add vanilla extract. Slowly add powdered sugar until buttercream reaches the desired consistency.
8. Pipe onto cooled cupcakes and top with a small slice of fresh peach.

Makes 20–24 cupcakes.

Churro Cupcakes

Cupcakes:
1 box white or yellow cake mix
½ tsp. nutmeg, optional
3 eggs
½ C. melted butter, cooled
¾ C. buttermilk
¾ C. sour cream
2 tsp. vanilla extract

Cinnamon Sugar Coating:
¼ C. sugar
1 T. cinnamon
Butter

Cinnamon Buttercream:
1 C. butter, softened
2 tsp. vanilla extract
4–5 C. powdered sugar
1 T. milk, if needed
Cinnamon sugar for garnish

Directions:

1. Preheat oven to 350 and line pans with cupcake liners.
2. Sift cake mix and nutmeg into a bowl; set aside.
3. In a large bowl, use a whisk to combine eggs, melted butter, buttermilk, sour cream, and vanilla extract until smooth.
4. Add cake mix and nutmeg mixture; stir until smooth.
5. Fill cupcake liners ¾ full and bake for 17–22 minutes or until a knife inserted near the center comes out clean.
6. For Cinnamon Sugar Coating: In a small bowl, combine sugar and cinnamon. As soon as the cupcakes are cool enough to hold in your hands, use a stick of butter to rim the edges of each cupcake (the butter should melt as it slides across); immediately roll the buttery rim in the cinnamon-sugar mixture. Repeat with each cupcake.
7. For Cinnamon Buttercream: Beat butter for 2 minutes. Scrape down the bowl and beat again while adding vanilla extract. Slowly add powdered sugar until buttercream reaches desired consistency. If the buttercream gets too thick, add milk.
8. Pipe onto cooled cupcakes and top with extra cinnamon sugar.

Makes 20–24 cupcakes.

Chocolate Banana Peanut Butter Cupcakes

Chocolate Banana Cupcakes:
1 box devil's food cake mix
¾ C. bananas, mashed
½ tsp. lemon juice
3 eggs
½ C. + 2 T. oil
½ C. milk or buttermilk
2 tsp. vanilla extract

Chocolate Ganache:
1 C. semisweet chocolate chips
¼ C. heavy whipping cream

Peanut Butter Buttercream:
½ C. smooth peanut butter
½ C. butter, softened
2 tsp. vanilla extract
4–5 C. powdered sugar
1–2 T. milk
Sprinkles, chocolate shavings, or chopped peanuts for garnish

Directions:

1. Preheat oven to 350 and line pans with cupcake liners.
2. Sift cake mix into a small bowl; set aside.
3. In a separate small bowl, mash bananas and lemon juice together; set aside.
4. In a large bowl, combine eggs, oil, buttermilk, and vanilla extract until smooth.
5. Add sifted cake mix and mashed bananas; stir to combine well.
6. Fill cupcake liners ¾ full and bake for 17–22 minutes or until a knife inserted near the center comes out clean. Let cool completely.
7. For Chocolate Ganache: In a microwave-safe bowl, combine chocolate chips and whipping cream; microwave for 15 seconds. Remove and stir; continue to microwave until smooth, stirring every 15 seconds. Be careful not to burn the chocolate.
8. Dip the top of a cooled cupcakes into the ganache. If the ganache starts to drip down the sides, you may want to let the ganache cool for a minute before dipping the rest of your cupcakes.
9. For Peanut Butter Buttercream: Beat peanut butter and butter for 2 minutes. Scrape down the sides of the bowl and add vanilla extract. Add 1 T. milk and slowly add powdered sugar until buttercream reaches desired consistency. If the buttercream becomes too thick, add an addition 1 T. milk.
10. Once the ganache on the cupcakes has cooled and become firm, pipe buttercream on top. Decorate with sprinkles, chocolate shavings, or peanuts.

Makes 20–24 cupcakes.

Chocolate Ice Cream Sundae Cupcakes

Chocolate Cupcakes:
1 box devil's food cake mix
3 eggs
½ C. oil
¾ C. buttermilk or milk
¾ C. sour cream
2 tsp. vanilla extract

Vanilla Cream Buttercream:
¾ C. butter, softened
4 oz. cream cheese, softened
2 tsp. vanilla extract
1½ T. whipping cream
4–5 C. powered sugar

Chocolate Ganache:
1 C. semisweet or milk chocolate chips
¼ C. whipping cream
1 T. honey
Sprinkles and cherries for garnish

Directions:

1. Preheat oven to 350 and line pans with cupcake liners.
2. Sift cake mix into a small bowl; set aside.
3. In a large bowl, combine eggs, oil, buttermilk, sour cream, and vanilla extract until smooth.
4. Stir in cake mix until well combined.
5. Fill cupcake liners ¾ full and bake for 17–22 minutes or until a knife inserted near the center comes out clean. Let cool completely.
6. For Vanilla Cream Buttercream: Beat butter and cream cheese for 2 minutes. Add vanilla extract and whipping cream and beat again. Slowly add powdered sugar until buttercream reaches desired consistency.
7. Pipe onto cooled cupcakes.
8. For Chocolate Ganache: Combine chocolate chips and whipping cream. On the stove top or in the microwave, melt until smooth; stir constantly to avoid burning. Add honey while stirring.
9. Spoon a small amount of chocolate ganache over each frosted cupcake; top with sprinkles and cherries.

Makes 20–24 cupcakes.

Dipped Cone Cupcakes

Chocolate Cupcakes:
20–24 small ice cream cones
1 box devil's food cake mix
3 eggs
½ C. oil
1 C. milk
½ C. sour cream
2 tsp. vanilla extract

Vanilla Buttercream:
1 C. butter, softened
2 tsp. vanilla extract
4–5 C. powdered sugar
1 T. milk, if needed

Chocolate Coating:
1½ C. candy dipping chocolate (see note)
Sprinkles for decoration

Directions:

1. Preheat oven to 350 and place an ice cream cone in each well of a cupcake pan.
2. Sift cake mix into a small bowl; set aside.
3. In a large bowl, combine eggs, oil, milk, sour cream, and vanilla extract.
4. Stir in cake mix until smooth.
5. Carefully fill ice cream cones with cake batter to about ½ inch from the top of each cone.
6. Bake for 17–22 minutes or until a knife inserted near the center comes out clean. Let cool completely.
7. For Vanilla Buttercream: Beat butter for 2 minutes; stir in vanilla extract. Slowly add powdered sugar until buttercream reaches desired consistency; it should be a little thicker than usual. Add 1 T. milk if it becomes too thick.
8. Pipe the buttercream onto each cooled cupcake.
9. For Chocolate Coating: On the stove top or in the microwave, melt chocolate until smooth, stirring constantly so it doesn't burn. Remove from heat.
10. Place chocolate in a tall container wide enough so you can dip the cones.
11. Submerge each frosted cone into the chocolate and remove immediately. The chocolate will run down the cupcake a little, so don't dip it all the way to the rim of the cone.
12. The chocolate will cool fast, so top with sprinkles immediately after dipping.

Note: Dipping chocolate is different from chocolate chips because it does not contain extra stabilizers. Pieces of dipping chocolate usually look like little disks.

Makes 20–24 cupcakes.

Strawberry Lime Cupcakes

Lime Cupcakes:
1 box white cake mix
4 egg whites
⅓ C. oil
¾ C. milk
¼ C. lime juice
¼ C. sour cream
2 T. lime zest

Strawberry Buttercream:
½ C. butter, softened
8 oz. cream cheese, softened
1 tsp. vanilla extract
4–5 C. powdered sugar
2–4 T. strawberry puree
2 tsp. strawberry-flavored gelatin, optional
Fresh lime slices for decoration

Directions:

1. Preheat oven to 350 and line pans with cupcake liners.
2. Sift cake mix into a small bowl; set aside.
3. In a large bowl, use a whisk to gently combine egg whites, oil, milk, lime juice, sour cream, and lime zest.
4. Add cake mix; stir until smooth.
5. Fill cupcake liners ¾ full and bake for 17–22 minutes or until a knife inserted near the center comes out clean.
6. For Strawberry Buttercream: Beat butter and cream cheese for 2 minutes. Scrape down the bowl, add vanilla extract, and beat again. Slowly add powdered sugar until buttercream is slightly thicker than desired. Slowly add strawberry puree (fresh strawberries that have been pureed in a blender) until buttercream reaches desired consistency. Add gelatin for additional color and flavor if desired.
7. Pipe onto cooled cupcakes and top with a slice of lime.

Makes 20–24 cupcakes.

Apple Cookie Dough Cupcakes

Apple Cupcakes:

1 box white or yellow cake mix

2 tsp. cinnamon or apple pie spice

3 eggs

2 T. oil

½ C. applesauce

¾ C. milk

¼ C. sour cream

2 tsp. vanilla extract

1 C. chopped apples (pieces should be about the size of marbles)

Cookie Dough Frosting:

1 C. butter, softened

2⅓ C. powdered sugar

⅓ + 2 T. brown sugar, packed

¾ C. flour

2 T. milk

2 tsp. vanilla extract

Fresh apple slices for decoration (see note)

Mini chocolate chips for garnish

Directions:

1. Preheat oven to 350 and line pans with cupcake liners.
2. Sift cake mix and cinnamon into a small bowl; set aside.
3. In a large bowl, use a whisk to gently combine eggs, oil, applesauce, milk, sour cream, and vanilla extract until smooth.
4. Add cake mix and cinnamon and stir until combined.
5. Fold in chopped apples.
6. Fill cupcake liners ¾ full and bake for 17–22 minutes or until a knife inserted near the center comes out clean. Let cool completely.
7. For Cookie Dough Frosting: Beat butter, powdered sugar, and brown sugar for 2 minutes. Add flour, milk, and vanilla extract; beat until smooth.
8. Pipe frosting onto cooled cupcakes; top with a slice of apple and mini chocolate chips.

Note: To keep apple slices from turning brown, dip them in lemon juice and wipe off excess juice before placing them on cupcakes.

Makes 20–24 cupcakes.

Cookies-and-Cream Cupcakes

Chocolate Cupcakes:
- 24 chocolate cookies with cream filling
- 1 box devil's food cake mix
- 3 eggs
- ½ C. oil
- ¾ C. buttermilk
- ¾ C. sour cream
- 2 tsp. vanilla extract

Cookies-and-Cream Butter cream:
- ½ C. butter, softened
- 8 oz. cream cheese, softened
- 2 tsp. vanilla extract
- 4–5 C. powdered sugar
- ⅓ C. cookie "powder" (see directions)
- 1 T. milk, if needed
- Extra chocolate cookies for decoration

Directions:

1. Preheat oven to 350 and line pans with cupcake liners.
2. Cookie preparation: Split 24 chocolate cookies in half so that only one side has the cream filling. Place one cream-side cookie in the bottom of each cupcake liner, cream side up. Put the cookie halves without cream in a food processor and pulverize them. Sift out any chunks. Set aside the cookie pieces that go through the sifter; they are the cookie "powder" that will be used in the buttercream.
3. Sift cake mix into a small bowl; set aside.
4. In a large bowl, use a whisk to combine the eggs, oil, buttermilk, sour cream, and vanilla extract.
5. Add cake mix; stir until smooth.
6. Fill cupcake liners ¾ full, placing batter on top of cream-side-up cookie halves; bake for 17–22 minutes or until a knife inserted near the center comes out clean. Let cool completely.
7. For Cookies-and-Cream Buttercream: Beat butter and cream cheese for 2 minutes. Add vanilla extract and slowly add powdered sugar until buttercream is a consistency slightly looser than what you want the final product to be. Fold in cookie "powder." Use milk to thin out the buttercream if needed.
8. Pipe onto cooled cupcakes and top with another cookie.

Makes 20–24 cupcakes.

All Dressed Up

Sometimes I feel like I live in the kitchen. My clothes are covered in powdered sugar, my hands are coated with butter, and my curls are too often embellished with frosting. Sometimes a girl just needs to get all dressed up for a night on the town. These are the cupcakes for just those occasions.

Chocolate Zucchini Cupcakes

Cupcakes:
1 box devil's food cake mix
1½ tsp. cinnamon
3 eggs
½ C. oil
¾ C. buttermilk
2 tsp. vanilla extract
2¾ C. zucchini, peeled and grated

Cinnamon Buttercream:
½ C. butter, softened
8 oz. cream cheese, softened
1½ tsp. cinnamon
4–5 C. powdered sugar
1 T. milk, if needed
Cinnamon and sugar for garnish

Note: Use Ateco #866 tip.

Directions:

1. Preheat oven to 350 and line pans with cupcake liners.
2. In a small bowl, sift cake mix and cinnamon; set aside.
3. In a large bowl, combine eggs, oil, buttermilk, and vanilla extract.
4. Add cake mix and stir until smooth.
5. Fold in grated zucchini.
6. Fill cupcake liners ¾ full and bake for 15–20 minutes or until a knife inserted near the center comes out clean.
7. For Cinnamon Buttercream: Beat butter and cream cheese for 2 minutes. Scrape down the bowl and beat again. Add cinnamon and slowly add powdered sugar until buttercream reaches desired consistency. Add milk if the buttercream becomes too thick.
8. Pipe buttercream onto cooled cupcakes and top with cinnamon and sugar.

Makes 24 cupcakes.

Chocolate Banana Cupcakes

Cupcakes:
1 box devil's food cake mix
2 tsp. cinnamon
1 C. mashed bananas
1 tsp. baking soda
3 eggs
½ C. + 2 T. oil
1 C. buttermilk
2 tsp. vanilla extract

Cinnamon Buttercream:
½ C. butter, softened
8 oz. cream cheese, softened
1½ tsp. cinnamon
4–5 C. powdered sugar
1 T. milk, if needed
Sliced banana for garnish

Note: Use Ateco #825 tip.

Directions:

1. Preheat oven to 350 and line pans with cupcake liners.
2. In a small bowl, sift cake mix and cinnamon; set aside.
3. In a separate small bowl, stir mashed bananas and baking soda; set aside.
4. In a large bowl, combine eggs, oil, buttermilk, and vanilla extract.
5. Add cake mix and mashed bananas. Stir until smooth.
6. Fill cupcake liners ¾ full and bake for 15–20 minutes or until a knife inserted near the center comes out clean.
7. For Cinnamon Buttercream: Beat butter and cream cheese for 2 minutes. Scrape down the bowl and beat again. Stir in cinnamon. Gradually add powdered sugar until buttercream reaches desired consistency. Add milk if the buttercream becomes too thick.
8. Pipe buttercream onto cooled cupcakes and finish with a slice of fresh banana.

Makes 24 cupcakes.

Chocolate Raspberry Cupcakes

Cupcakes:
1 box devil's food cake mix
3 eggs
½ C. oil
¾ C. buttermilk
½ C. sour cream
2 tsp. vanilla extract
1⅓ C. fresh raspberries

Raspberry Buttercream:
1.2-oz. pkg. freeze-dried raspber ries
1 C. butter, softened
4–5 C. powdered sugar
1 T. milk, if needed
Fresh raspberries for garnish

Note: Use Ateco #846 tip.

Directions:

1. Preheat oven to 350 and line pans with cupcake liners.
2. Sift cake mix into a small bowl; set aside.
3. In a large bowl, use a whisk to combine eggs, oil, buttermilk, sour cream, and vanilla extract.
4. Add cake mix and stir until smooth.
5. Fold in raspberries. (If the raspberries are large, roughly chop them before adding them to the batter.)
6. Fill cupcake liners ¾ full and bake for 15–20 minutes or until a knife inserted near the center comes out clean.
7. For Raspberry Buttercream: Pulverize freeze-dried raspberries in a food processor; using a fine sifter, sift out and discard the seeds. Set pulverized raspberries aside.
8. Beat butter for 2 minutes. Scrape down the sides of the bowl, add pulverized freeze-dried raspberries, and beat again. Slowly add powdered sugar until buttercream is the desired consistency. Add milk if the buttercream becomes too stiff.
9. Pipe buttercream onto cooled cupcakes and top with a fresh raspberry.

Makes 24 cupcakes.

Banana Nut Maple Cupcakes

Banana Nut Cupcakes:
1 box white cake mix
1 C. bananas, mashed
1 tsp. baking soda
3 eggs
½ C. oil
¾ C. milk
2 tsp. vanilla extract
1¼ C. walnuts, chopped

Maple Buttercream:
½ C. butter, softened
8 oz. cream cheese, softened
1 tsp. vanilla extract
2 tsp. maple flavoring
3–4 C. powdered sugar
1 T. milk, if needed
Chopped walnuts for garnish

Note: Use Wilton 2D tip.

Directions:

1. Preheat oven to 350 and line pans with cupcake liners.
2. Sift cake mix into a small bowl; set aside.
3. In another small bowl, stir mashed bananas and baking soda. Set aside.
4. In a large bowl, combine eggs, oil, milk, and vanilla extract.
5. Add cake mix and mashed bananas to wet ingredients and mix until smooth.
6. Fold in walnuts.
7. Fill cupcake liners ¾ full and bake for 15–20 minutes or until a knife inserted near the center comes out clean.
8. For Maple Buttercream: Beat butter and cream cheese for two minutes. Scrape down the bowl and beat again. Add vanilla and maple flavoring; gradually add powdered sugar until buttercream reaches desired consistency. If it becomes too thick, add milk.
9. Pipe buttercream onto cooled cupcakes and top with more chopped walnuts.

Makes 24 cupcakes.

Orange White Chocolate Cupcakes

Orange Cupcakes:
1 box white cake mix
4 egg whites
⅓ C. oil
⅓ C. orange juice
¾ C. buttermilk
Zest of 3 oranges

White Chocolate Ganache:
1 C. white chocolate chips
3 T. whipping cream

Orange Buttercream:
1 C. butter, softened
Zest of 2 oranges
1 T. orange juice
3–4 C. powdered sugar
Pieces of white chocolate for garnish

Note: Use Ateco #809 tip.

Directions:

1. Preheat oven to 350 and line pans with cupcake liners.
2. Sift cake mix into a small bowl; set aside.
3. In a large bowl, combine egg whites, oil, orange juice, buttermilk, and zest of 3 oranges.
4. Add cake mix and stir until smooth.
5. Fill cupcake liners ¾ full and bake for 15–20 minutes or until a knife inserted near the center comes out clean. Cool completely.
6. For Ganache: Place white chocolate chips and whipping cream in a heatproof bowl and melt over the stove (at low heat) or in the microwave; stir constantly until smooth.
7. Dip the tops of cooled cupcakes in the ganache. If the ganache drips onto the liner, let the ganache cool a little so it becomes thicker.
8. For Orange Buttercream: Beat butter until smooth. Add the zest of 2 oranges and the orange juice and beat again. Add powdered sugar gradually until the buttercream is the desired consistency. If it becomes too thick, add more orange juice.
9. After the ganache has set, pipe buttercream on top and finish with white chocolate pieces.

Makes 24 cupcakes.

Lemon Blueberry Cupcakes

Lemon Blueberry Cupcakes:
1 box white cake mix
4 egg whites
⅓ C. oil
¼ C. lemon juice
½ C. milk
⅓ C. plain or vanilla yogurt
Zest of 2 lemons
1½ C. blueberries, fresh or frozen
1½ tsp. flour

Lemon Cream:
½ C. butter, softened
8 oz. cream cheese, softened
Zest of 2 lemons
1 T. lemon juice
3–4 C. powdered sugar
Fresh blueberries for garnish
Sprinkles for garnish

Note: Use Ateco #846 tip.

Directions:

1. Preheat oven to 350 and line pans with cupcake liners.
2. Sift cake mix into a small bowl; set aside.
3. In a large bowl, use a whisk to combine egg whites, oil, lemon juice, milk, yogurt, and zest of 2 lemons.
4. Add cake mix to liquid ingredients and stir until combined.
5. In a small bowl, gently coat blueberries in flour.
6. Add blueberries to batter and fold in.
7. Fill cupcake liners ¾ full and bake for 20–25 minutes or until a knife inserted near the center comes out clean.
8. For Lemon Cream: Beat butter and cream cheese for 2 minutes. Scrape down the bowl, add zest of 2 lemons, and beat again. Add lemon juice. Gradually add powdered sugar until cream reaches the desired consistency.
9. Pipe lemon cream onto cooled cupcakes and top with fresh blueberries and sprinkles.

Makes 24–30 cupcakes.

Chocolate Coconut Cupcakes

Chocolate Cupcakes:
1 box devil's food cake mix
3 eggs
½ C. oil
1 C. buttermilk
1 C. sour cream
2 tsp. vanilla extract

Coconut Cream:
8 oz. cream cheese, softened
½ C. butter, softened
2 tsp. coconut extract
1 tsp. vanilla extract
3–4 C. powdered sugar
1 T. milk, if needed
Shredded coconut for garnish

Directions:

1. Preheat oven to 350 and line pans with cupcake liners.
2. Sift cake mix into a small bowl; set aside.
3. In a large bowl, use a whisk to combine eggs, oil, buttermilk, sour cream, and vanilla extract. Mix until smooth.
4. Add cake mix and stir well.
5. Fill cupcake liners ¾ full and bake for 16–20 minutes or until a knife inserted near the center comes out clean.
6. For Coconut Cream: Beat cream cheese and butter for 2 minutes. Scrape down the bowl and beat again. Add coconut extract and vanilla extract. Gradually add powdered sugar until the cream reaches desired consistency. If it becomes too thick, use milk to thin it.
7. Frost cooled cupcakes and roll top of each cupcake in shredded coconut to coat.

Makes 24 cupcakes.

Blackberry White Chocolate Cupcakes

Blackberry Vanilla Cupcakes:
1 box white cake mix
3 eggs
⅓ C. oil
1¼ C. milk
2 tsp. vanilla extract
1½ C. fresh blackberries

White Chocolate Ganache:
1 C. white chocolate chips
3 T. whipping cream

Blackberry Buttercream:
1 C. butter, softened
2 T. blackberry puree, strained
3–4 C. powdered sugar
Fresh blackberries for garnish

Directions:

1. Preheat oven to 350 and line pans with cupcake liners.
2. Sift cake mix into a small bowl; set aside.
3. In a large bowl, combine eggs, oil, milk, and vanilla extract.
4. Add cake mix and stir until smooth.
5. Fold in blackberries. (If the blackberries are large, cut in half before adding to batter.)
6. Fill cupcake liners ¾ full and bake for 16–20 minutes or until a knife inserted near the center comes out clean.
7. For White Chocolate Ganache: Place white chocolate chips in a heatproof bowl. In a small saucepan, heat whipping cream until bubbles start to form around the edges. Pour hot cream over white chocolate chips and stir until smooth.
8. Dip the tops of cooled cupcakes into the ganache and let set, or spoon the ganache over the tops of the cupcakes.
9. For Blackberry Buttercream: Beat butter for 2 minutes. Scrape down the sides of the bowl, add blackberry puree, and beat again. Gradually add powdered sugar until the buttercream reaches the desired consistency.
10. Pipe buttercream on top of the cupcakes once the ganache is firm to the touch. Top with a fresh blackberry.

Note: To make blackberry puree, place blackberries in a blender or food processor and blend until liquid. Put the puree through a strainer to remove all seeds.

Makes 24 cupcakes.

Neapolitan Cupcakes

Chocolate Cake:
1 box devil's food cake mix
3 eggs
½ C. oil
1 C. milk
⅓ C. sour cream
2 tsp. vanilla extract

Vanilla Cake:
1 box white cake mix
3 eggs
⅓ C. oil
1 C. milk
1/3 C. sour cream
1 T. vanilla extract

Strawberry Buttercream:
2 C. butter, softened
¼ C. strawberry puree
2 tsp. vanilla extract
6–8 C. powdered sugar
Fresh strawberries for garnish

Note: Use Ateco #826 tip.

Directions:

1. Preheat oven to 350 and line pans with cupcake liners.
2. Sift each cake mix into a separate bowl; set aside.
3. For Chocolate Cake: In a large bowl, combine eggs, oil, milk, sour cream, and vanilla extract. Add sifted devil's food cake mix; stir until smooth.
4. For Vanilla Cake: In a separate large bowl, combine eggs, oil, milk, sour cream, and vanilla extract. Add sifted white cake mix; stir until smooth.
5. Place a small scoop of chocolate batter in the side of each cupcake liner. Place a small scoop of vanilla batter next to the chocolate in each cupcake liner.
6. Bake for 16–20 minutes or until a knife inserted near the center comes out clean.
7. For Strawberry Buttercream: Beat butter for 2 minutes, scrape down the bowl, and beat again. Add strawberry puree and vanilla extract. Gradually add powdered sugar until the buttercream reaches the desired consistency.
8. Pipe buttercream onto cooled cupcakes and top with a fresh strawberry.

Makes 48 cupcakes.

Chocolate Chili Cupcakes

Chocolate Cupcakes:
1 box devil's food cake mix
3 eggs
½ C. oil
1 C. buttermilk
½ C. sour cream
2 tsp. vanilla extract
2 tsp. cinnamon

Spicy Buttercream:
½ C. butter, softened
8 oz. cream cheese
1 tsp. vanilla extract
3–4 C. powdered sugar
1–2 tsp. cayenne pepper
Milk, if needed

Directions:

1. Preheat oven to 350 and line pans with cupcake liners.
2. Sift cake mix into a small bowl; set aside.
3. In a large bowl, use a whisk to combine eggs, oil, buttermilk, sour cream, vanilla extract, and cinnamon.
4. Add cake mix and stir until smooth.
5. Fill cupcake liners ¾ full and bake for 16–20 minutes or until a knife inserted near the center comes out clean.
6. For Spicy Buttercream: Beat butter and cream cheese for 2 minutes, scrape down the bowl, and beat again. Add vanilla extract and slowly add powdered sugar until buttercream is the desired consistency. Add a little cayenne at a time (taste along the way so you don't go overboard). Once the buttercream is as spicy as desired, add a little milk if needed to thin it.
7. Pipe buttercream onto cooled cupcakes and dust with cinnamon and cayenne pepper.

Makes 24 cupcakes.

Chocolate Lemon Cupcakes

Chocolate Cupcakes:
1 box devil's food cake mix
3 eggs
½ C. oil
¾ C. buttermilk
½ C. sour cream
2 tsp. vanilla extract

Lemon Glaze:
1 C. powdered sugar
2 T. lemon juice
Zest of 1 lemon

Lemon Cream:
½ C. butter, softened
8 oz. cream cheese
Zest of 2 lemons
1 T. lemon juice
3–4 C. powdered sugar
Yellow sprinkles for garnish

Directions:

1. Preheat oven to 350 and line pans with cupcake liners.
2. Sift cake mix into a small bowl; set aside.
3. In a large bowl, combine eggs, oil, buttermilk, sour cream, and vanilla extract.
4. Add cake mix and stir until smooth.
5. Fill cupcake liners ¾ full and bake for 16–20 minutes or until a knife inserted near the center comes out clean. Cool cupcakes completely.
6. For Lemon Glaze: Combine powdered sugar, lemon juice, and lemon zest. Stir until smooth.
7. Spoon a little lemon glaze on top of each cooled cupcake. Let set.
8. For Lemon Cream: Beat butter and cream cheese for 2 minutes. Scrape down the bowl, add lemon zest, and beat again. Add lemon juice and slowly add powdered sugar until buttercream is the desired consistency.
9. Pipe buttercream on cupcake over the set glaze. Top with yellow sprinkles.

Makes 24 cupcakes.

Stuffed and Filled

"Don't tell Mom, Lizzy." My brother Paul made me promise not to tell her. I was four, and it was the first secret I ever kept. I remember being so proud that I was my brother's partner in crime and that I didn't tell Mom. But I only kept the secret because I didn't know what I wasn't supposed to tell. These cupcakes are the same—each has a secret of its own.

Cookies-and-Cream-Filled Cupcakes

Cookies-and-Cream Cupcakes:

- 24 chocolate cream-filled cookies
- 1 box devil's food cake mix
- ½ C. oil
- 3 eggs
- ¾ C. milk
- ½ C. sour cream
- 1 tsp. vanilla extract

Filling:

- 8 oz. cream cheese, softened
- ¼ C. butter, softened
- 3–4 C. powdered sugar
- Remaining chocolate cookies from cake

Chocolate Ganache:

- 1 C. chocolate chips
- ¼ C. heavy whipping cream
- ½ tsp. vanilla extract
- Melted white chocolate for decoration

Directions:

1. Preheat oven to 350 and line pans with cupcake liners.
2. Prepare cookies by twisting them to split them in half; all the cream filling should be on one half only. Place a half with cream in each cupcake liner, cream-side up. Save the halves without cream for the filling.
3. Sift cake mix into a small bowl; set aside.
4. In a large bowl, combine oil, eggs, milk, sour cream, and vanilla extract.
5. Stir in cake mix until smooth.
6. Scooping batter on top of cookies halves, fill cupcake liners ¾ full and bake for 16–22 minutes or until a knife inserted near the center comes out clean. Let cool completely.
7. For Filling: Combine cream cheese, butter, and powdered sugar; beat until smooth. Using a food processor, finely crush the remaining cookie halves. Stir into butter and cream cheese mixture until incorporated.
8. Using a small knife, cut a cone out of the top of each cooled cupcake and fill the hole with filling. Snip the tip off of the "cone" you cut out and place the top of the cone over the filling like a lid.
9. For Chocolate Ganache: In the microwave or over the stove, heat chocolate chips and cream and stir until smooth. Stir in vanilla extract.
10. Dip the tops of the cupcakes into the ganache (or spoon the ganache over the cupcakes). If the ganache runs down the liner, let the ganache cool a little more—it will thicken as it cools.
11. Drizzle melted white chocolate over the top for decoration.

Makes 24 cupcakes.

Banana Cupcakes with Chocolate Hazelnut Centers

Banana Cupcakes:
¾ C. mashed bananas
½ tsp. lemon juice
1 box yellow cake mix
½ tsp. cinnamon
3 eggs
⅓ C. oil
¾ C. milk
½ C. sour cream or plain yogurt
2 tsp. vanilla extract
¾ C. chocolate hazelnut spread

Chocolate Hazelnut Buttercream:
½ C. butter
½ C. chocolate hazelnut spread
1 tsp. vanilla extract
1–2 T. milk
4–5 C. powdered sugar
Sprinkles for garnish

Directions:

1. Preheat oven to 350 and line pans with cupcake liners.
2. In a small bowl, use a fork to finely mash bananas with lemon juice; set aside.
3. Sift cake mix and cinnamon together into a separate bowl; set aside.
4. In a large bowl, combine eggs, oil, milk, sour cream, and vanilla extract until smooth.
5. Stir in cake mix/cinnamon and mashed bananas; mix until well combined.
6. Fill cupcake liners ¾ full.
7. Drop about 1½ tsp. hazelnut spread on top of every mound of batter. Using a toothpick, push the spread down into the batter (not all the way to the bottom). If desired, you can also swirl it into the batter a little bit for decoration.
8. Bake for 17–22 minutes or until a knife inserted toward the side comes out clean. Don't insert the knife into the cream center, because the spread will still be a little gooey.
9. For Chocolate Hazelnut Buttercream: Beat butter and hazelnut spread for 2 minutes. Add vanilla extract and 1 T. milk. Slowly add powdered sugar until buttercream reaches desired consistency. If it becomes too thick, add enough milk to create a creamy consistency.
10. Pipe buttercream onto cooled cupcakes and top with sprinkles.

Makes 24 cupcakes.

Pineapple Inside-Out Cupcakes

Pineapple Cupcakes:
1 box yellow cake mix
3 eggs
½ C. oil
¾ C. crushed pineapple, drained
½ C. milk
1 tsp. vanilla extract
24 maraschino cherries, stems removed

Brown Sugar Glaze:
½ C. light brown sugar, packed
½ tsp. vanilla extract
2 T. hot water
Powdered sugar, optional
Extra maraschino cherries for decoration

Directions:

1. Preheat oven to 350 and line pans with cupcake liners.
2. Sift cake mix into a small bowl; set aside.
3. In a large bowl, combine eggs, oil, pineapple, milk, and vanilla extract.
4. Add cake mix; stir until smooth.
5. Fill cupcake liners 2/3 full; press a maraschino cherry into the center of the batter for each cupcake.
6. Bake for 17–22 minutes or until a knife inserted toward the side comes out clean.
7. For Brown Sugar Glaze: Combine all ingredients until smooth. If you want the glaze thicker, add powdered sugar 1 T. at a time until the glaze is the desired consistency.
8. Spoon glaze over cupcakes. (If desired, you can poke the cupcake with a toothpick first to allow room for the glaze can sink into the holes.)
9. Top with a maraschino cherry.

Makes 24 cupcakes.

Chocolate Hazelnut Cupcakes

Chocolate Hazelnut Cupcakes:
1 box devil's food cake mix
1 3.4-oz. pkg. chocolate instant pudding mix
4 eggs
2/3 C. oil
1 C. buttermilk
½ C. sour cream
1 tsp. vanilla extract
¾ C. chocolate hazelnut spread

Chocolate Hazelnut Buttercream:
½ C. butter, softened
½ C. chocolate hazelnut spread
1–2 T. milk
1 tsp. vanilla extract
4–5 C. powdered sugar
Chopped hazelnuts for garnish

Directions:

1. Preheat oven to 350 and line pans with cupcake liners.
2. Sift cake mix and instant pudding mix into a small bowl; set aside.
3. In a large bowl, combine eggs, oil, buttermilk, sour cream, and vanilla extract.
4. Add cake/pudding mixture; stir until smooth.
5. Fill cupcake liners 2/3 full.
6. Place a 1½-tsp. dollop of hazelnut spread on top of each mound of batter. Use a toothpick to gently press the dollop into the center of the batter.
7. Bake for 17–22 minutes or until a knife inserted near the side comes out clean. (The spread in the center may still be gooey.)
8. For Chocolate Hazelnut Buttercream: Beat butter and hazelnut spread. Add 1 T. milk and vanilla extract. Slowly add powdered sugar until buttercream reaches desired consistency. If the buttercream gets too thick, add more milk to achieve a creamy consistency.
9. Pipe onto cooled cupcakes and top with chopped hazelnuts.

Makes 24 cupcakes.

Coconut Pineapple Cupcakes

Pineapple Filling:
½ C. sugar
4 T. flour
1 pinch salt
1 egg
1 C. crushed pineapple, drained
¾ C. pineapple juice
1 tsp. cornstarch
2 T. butter

Coconut Cupcakes:
1 box white cake mix
4 egg whites
⅓ C. oil
1 C. coconut milk
⅓ C. plain yogurt
2 tsp. coconut extract
1 tsp. vanilla extract

Coconut Cream Frosting:
8 oz. cream cheese, softened
½ C. butter, softened
1½ tsp. coconut extract
3–4 C. powdered sugar
Toasted coconut for garnish

Directions:

1. For Pineapple Filling: In the top of a double boiler, combine sugar, flour, salt, egg, crushed pineapple, pineapple juice, and cornstarch. Heat over medium-high heat until thickened, stirring constantly. Remove from heat, add butter, and let cool. Refrigerate until needed.
2. Preheat oven to 350 and line pans with cupcake liners.
3. Sift cake mix into a small bowl; set aside.
4. In a large bowl, combine eggs, oil, coconut milk, yogurt, coconut extract, and vanilla extract.
5. Stir in cake mix until smooth.
6. Fill cupcake liners ¾ full and bake for 17–22 minutes or until a knife inserted near the center comes out clean. Let cool completely.
7. For Coconut Cream Frosting: Beat cream cheese and butter. Stir in coconut extract and slowly add powdered sugar until frosting is the desired consistency. If the frosting becomes too thick, add 1 T. milk.
8. To assemble: Using a small knife, cut a "cone" shape out of the top of each cooled cupcake. Discard the "cones." Fill the holes with cooled pineapple filling. Pipe coconut cream over the top and roll in toasted coconut.

Makes 24 cupcakes.

Raspberry Lemon Cheesecake Cupcakes

Lemon Cupcakes:
1 box white cake mix
4 egg whites
⅓ C. oil
¾ C. buttermilk
¼ C. lemon juice
2 T. lemon zest

Cheesecake Filling:
8 oz. cream cheese, softened
¾ C. powdered sugar

Raspberry Buttercream:
½ C. butter, softened
8 oz. cream cheese, softened
3–4 T. raspberry puree
4–5 C. powdered sugar
Fresh raspberries for decoration

Directions:

1. Preheat oven to 350 and line pans with cupcake liners.
2. Sift cake mix into a small bowl; set aside.
3. In a large bowl, combine egg whites, oil, buttermilk, lemon juice, and lemon zest.
4. Add cake mix; stir until smooth.
5. Fill cupcake liners ¾ full.
6. For Cheesecake Filling: Combine cream cheese and powdered sugar; beat until smooth. Place a 1½-tsp. dollop in the center of each mound of batter. Use a toothpick to push the filling a little bit into the batter.
7. Bake for 17–22 minutes or until a knife inserted toward the side comes out clean. (The filling at the center may still be gooey.)
8. For Raspberry Buttercream: Beat butter and cream cheese. Add 2 T. raspberry puree (process fresh raspberries in a blender; press through a sieve to remove seeds). Slowly add powdered sugar until buttercream reaches desired consistency. If the buttercream gets too thick, add a little raspberry puree.
9. Pipe buttercream onto cooled cupcakes and top with fresh raspberries.

Makes 24 cupcakes.

Chocolate Mascarpone Cupcakes

Chocolate Cupcakes:
1 box devil's food cake mix
1 tsp. cinnamon
3 eggs
½ C. oil
¾ C. buttermilk
½ C. plain yogurt or sour cream
1 tsp. vanilla extract

Mascarpone Filling:
8 oz. mascarpone cheese
1 tsp. vanilla extract
½ C. powdered sugar

Chocolate Buttercream:
½ C. butter, softened
8 oz. cream cheese, softened
1 tsp. vanilla extract
¾ C. unsweetened cocoa
3–4 C. powdered sugar
1 T. milk, if needed
Sprinkles for garnish

Directions:

1. Preheat oven to 350 and line pans with cupcake liners.
2. Sift cake mix and cinnamon into a small bowl; set aside.
3. In a large bowl, combine eggs, oil, buttermilk, yogurt, and vanilla extract.
4. Add cake mix/cinnamon mixture; stir until smooth.
5. Fill cupcake liners ¾ full and bake for 17–22 minutes or until a knife inserted near the center comes out clean. Let cool completely.
6. For Mascarpone Filling: Mix mascarpone cheese, vanilla extract, and powdered sugar until smooth.
7. Using a knife, cut a little "cone" out of the top of each cooled cupcake; discard the "cones." Fill each hole generously with mascarpone filling.
8. For Chocolate Buttercream: Beat butter and cream cheese. Stir in vanilla extract and cocoa. Slowly add powdered sugar until buttercream reaches the desired consistency. If it becomes too thick, add milk to make the mixture creamy and light.
9. Pipe buttercream over the mascarpone filling and top with sprinkles.

Makes 24 cupcakes.

Cherry Pie Cupcakes

Cherry Cupcakes:

1 box white cake mix

1/3 C. butter, melted and cooled

3 eggs

1 C. buttermilk

1 1/2 tsp. almond extract

1 tsp. vanilla extract

24 cherries, pitted and stems removed

Graham Cracker Buttercream:

1/4 C. graham crackers, finely crushed

1 C. butter, softened

1 tsp. vanilla extract

1–2 T. milk

3–4 C. powdered sugar

Red chocolate candies for decoration

Directions:

1. Preheat oven to 350 and line pans with cupcake liners.
2. Sift cake mix into a small bowl; set aside.
3. In a large bowl, combine melted butter, eggs, buttermilk, almond extract, and vanilla extract.
4. Stir in cake mix until smooth.
5. Fill cupcake liners 3/4 full and press a cherry into the center of each mound of batter.
6. Bake for 17–22 minutes or until a knife inserted toward the side comes out clean.
7. For Graham Cracker Buttercream: Using a food processor, finely crush graham crackers; use a sifter to sift out the larger pieces. Discard the larger pieces. In a stand mixer, beat butter and vanilla extract. Add crushed graham crackers and 1 T. milk. Slowly add powdered sugar until buttercream reaches desired consistency. If the buttercream becomes too thick, add more milk.
8. Once cupcakes have cooled, cut the tops off to create a flat surface. Using a knife, spread a layer of buttercream on each cupcake then place red candies on the buttercream. Using a small round tip, pipe stripes of buttercream across the top to resemble a lattice crust; use a slightly larger tip to make the "crust" around the outside.

Makes 24 cupcakes.

Chocolate Chip Cookie Dough Cupcakes

Cupcakes:
1 box white or yellow cake mix
3 eggs
⅓ C. melted butter, cooled
1¼ C. buttermilk
2 tsp. vanilla extract

Chocolate Chip Filling:
¼ C. butter, softened
⅓ C. brown sugar, packed
1¼ C. flour
½ C. sweetened condensed milk
1 tsp. vanilla extract
⅓ C. mini chocolate chips

Cookie Dough Frosting:
1 C. butter, softened
½ C. brown sugar, packed
2/3 C. flour
½ tsp. salt
2 tsp. vanilla extract
2 tsp. milk
2–3 C. powdered sugar
Mini chocolate chips for decoration

Directions:

1. Preheat oven to 350 and line pans with cupcake liners.
2. Sift cake mix into a small bowl; set aside.
3. In a large bowl, combine eggs, melted butter, buttermilk, and vanilla extract.
4. Add cake mix and stir until smooth.
5. Fill cupcake liners ¾ full and bake for 17–22 minutes or until a knife inserted near the center comes out clean. Cool completely.
6. For Chocolate Chip Filling: Combine all ingredients except chocolate chips and mix until smooth. Stir in chocolate chips.
7. For Cookie Dough Frosting: Beat butter, brown sugar, flour, salt, vanilla extract, and milk. Slowly add powdered sugar until frosting reaches desired consistency. Add more milk a little at a time if the frosting is too stiff.
8. To assemble: Use a small knife to cut a "cone" out of the top of each cupcake. Generously fill the hole with a spoonful of filling and discard the "cone." Pipe frosting over the cupcake and garnish with mini chocolate chips.

Makes 24 cupcakes.

'Tis the Season for Cupcakes

If you walk into my pantry you will see about twenty cans of pumpkin puree on the left. It wasn't on sale, and I didn't buy it in bulk. I bought it because I heard on the news there was going to be a shortage of canned pumpkin—so I went to the grocery store that very night and bought all the cans I could find. I was not about to let some silly flood get in the way of me and my pumpkin desserts during the holidays. Turns out, there was no major shortage, and I am still working through my pumpkin stash. But when it comes to holidays and desserts, better be safe than sorry!

Pumpkin Pie Cupcakes

Pumpkin Cupcakes:

1 box spice cake mix (or yellow/white cake mix plus 1½ T. pumpkin pie spice)

3 eggs

½ C. applesauce

1 tsp. vanilla extract

¼ C. milk

1 15-oz. can pumpkin puree

Whipped Topping:

8 oz. cream cheese, softened

1 C. powdered sugar

1 tsp. vanilla extract

1 pint heavy whipping cream

Cinnamon or pumpkin pie spice for garnish

Directions:

1. Preheat oven to 350 and line pans with cupcake liners.
2. Sift cake mix into a small bowl; set aside.
3. In a large bowl, combine eggs, applesauce, vanilla, milk, and pumpkin puree until smooth.
4. Add cake mix; stir until combined well.
5. Fill cupcake liners ¾ full and bake for 17–22 minutes or until a knife inserted near the center comes out clean.
6. For Whipped Topping: Using a stand mixer with a paddle attachment, beat cream cheese and powdered sugar until smooth. Scrape down the sides of the bowl as needed. Switch to the whisk attachment and add vanilla and whipping cream; beat until stiff peaks form.
7. Pipe onto cooled cupcakes; sprinkle with cinnamon or pumpkin pie spice.

Makes 24 cupcakes.

Cranberry White Chocolate Cupcakes

Cranberry Cupcakes:
1 box white cake mix
2 egg whites
2 eggs
⅓ C. oil
¾ C. buttermilk
½ C. sour cream
Zest of 1 orange
2 C. chopped cranberries

White Chocolate Ganache:
1 C. white chocolate chips
3 T. heavy whipping cream

White Chocolate Buttercream:
8 oz. cream cheese, softened
½ C. butter, softened
2 T. white chocolate instant pudding mix (can also use cheesecake instant pudding)
1 tsp. vanilla extract
3–4 C. powdered sugar
Sprinkles for garnish

Directions:

1. Preheat oven to 350 and line pans with cupcake liners.
2. Sift cake mix into a small bowl; set aside.
3. In a large bowl, combine egg whites, eggs, oil, buttermilk, sour cream, and vanilla extract.
4. Add cake mix and stir until smooth.
5. Stir in orange zest and chopped cranberries.
6. Fill cupcake liners ¾ full and bake for 17–22 minutes or until a knife inserted near the center comes out clean.
7. For Ganache: In the microwave or on the stove top, melt white chocolate chips and cream until smooth. Stir constantly and use low heat—white chocolate burns easily. (If you live in a hot climate, you may need to add extra chocolate chips to make the ganache thick enough.)
8. Once cupcakes have cooled, dip the tops of the cupcakes into the ganache; let set. Dip one cupcake as a test; if the ganache runs down the sides, let the ganache cool longer. Let ganache set completely on cupcakes.
9. For White Chocolate Buttercream: Beat cream cheese and butter. Add instant pudding and vanilla extract. Slowly add powdered sugar until buttercream reaches desired consistency.
10. Pipe onto cupcakes and finish with sprinkles.

Makes 24 cupcakes.

Chocolate Peppermint Swirl Cupcakes

Chocolate Peppermint Cupcakes:
1 box devil's food cake mix
3 eggs
½ C. butter, melted and cooled
1 C. milk
1 tsp. vanilla extract
⅓ C. sour cream, optional

Peppermint Swirl Buttercream:
1 C. butter, softened
1½ tsp. peppermint extract
3–4 C. powdered sugar
1 T. milk, optional
Red gel or paste food dye (not liquid)
Crushed peppermint candies for garnish

Directions:

1. Preheat oven to 350 and line pans with cupcake liners.
2. Sift cake mix into a small bowl; set aside.
3. In a large bowl, combine eggs, butter, milk, vanilla extract, and sour cream.
4. Stir in cake mix until smooth.
5. Fill cupcake liners ¾ full and bake for 17–22 minutes or until a knife inserted near the center comes out clean.
6. For Peppermint Swirl Buttercream: Beat butter for 1 minute. Stir in peppermint extract; slowly add powdered sugar until buttercream reaches desired consistency. Add milk if the buttercream becomes too thick.
7. Place a round tip inside a piping bag. Using a toothpick, make 3 or 4 lines of red dye about 5 inches long on the inside of the bag, going from the top of the piping tip and up the bag.
8. Carefully fill bag with buttercream and pipe onto cooled cupcakes. Top with crushed peppermint candies.

Makes 24 cupcakes.

Chocolate Orange Cupcakes

Chocolate Cupcakes:
1 box devil's food cake mix
3 eggs
½ C. oil
¾ C. milk
½ C. sour cream
2 tsp. vanilla extract
1 C. mini chocolate chips

Dark Chocolate Ganache:
1 C. dark chocolate chips
¼ C. heavy whipping cream

Orange Buttercream:
1 C. butter, softened
Zest of 2 oranges
1 T. orange juice
3–4 C. powdered sugar
Sprinkles for decoration

Directions:

1. Preheat oven to 350 and line pans with cupcake liners.
2. Sift cake mix into a small bowl; set aside.
3. In a large bowl, combine eggs, oil, milk, sour cream, and vanilla extract.
4. Add cake mix and stir until smooth.
5. Add chocolate chips and stir again.
6. Fill cupcake liners ¾ full and bake for 17–22 minutes or until a knife inserted near the center comes out clean. Let cool completely.
7. For Dark Chocolate Ganache: In the microwave or on the stove top, melt chocolate chips and whipping cream until smooth. Stir frequently so it doesn't burn.
8. Dip the top of each cooled cupcake into the ganache. The ganache should not run down the sides of the liner; if it does, let the ganache cool a little longer.
9. For Orange Buttercream: Beat butter and orange zest for 2 minutes. Stir in orange juice. Slowly add powdered sugar until buttercream reaches desired consistency.
10. Once the ganache has set, pipe buttercream on top and finish with sprinkles.

Makes 24 cupcakes.

Red Velvet Cupcakes

Red Velvet Cupcakes:
1 box white cake mix
3 T. unsweetened cocoa powder
3 eggs
⅓ C. oil
¾ C. buttermilk
½ C. plain yogurt
2 tsp. vanilla extract
Red food dye
1 T. apple cider vinegar

Cream Cheese Frosting:
8 oz. cream cheese, softened
½ C. butter, softened
2 tsp. vanilla extract
3–4 C. powdered sugar

Directions:

1. Preheat oven to 350 and line pans with cupcake liners.
2. Sift cake mix and cocoa powder into a small bowl; set aside.
3. In a large bowl, combine eggs, oil, buttermilk, yogurt, and vanilla extract.
4. Stir in cake mix until smooth.
5. Add as much food dye as you'd like.
6. Once the batter is the desired color, stir in vinegar.
7. Fill cupcake liners ¾ full and bake for 17–22 minutes or until a knife inserted near the center comes out clean.
8. For Cream Cheese Frosting: Beat cream cheese and butter for 2 minutes. Add vanilla extract. Slowly add powdered sugar until frosting reaches desired consistency.
9. Pipe frosting onto cooled cupcakes in the shape of roses.

Makes 24 cupcakes.

Fruity Fourth Cupcakes

Vanilla Cupcakes:
1 box white cake mix
4 egg whites
⅓ C. oil
1 C. milk
⅓ C. mayonnaise
2 tsp. vanilla extract

Cream Cheese Frosting:
8 oz. cream cheese, softened
½ C. butter, softened
2 tsp. vanilla extract
3–4 C. powdered sugar
Raspberries, blueberries, and strawberries for decoration

Directions:

1. Preheat oven to 350 and line pans with cupcake liners.
2. Sift cake mix into a small bowl; set aside.
3. In a large bowl, combine egg whites, oil, milk, mayonnaise, and vanilla extract.
4. Stir in cake mix until smooth.
5. Fill cupcake liners ¾ full and bake for 17–22 minutes or until a knife inserted near the center comes out clean.
6. For Cream Cheese Frosting: Beat cream cheese and butter. Add vanilla extract. Slowly add powdered sugar until frosting reaches desired consistency.
7. Pipe onto cooled cupcakes; top with berries.

Makes 24 cupcakes.

Chocolate Pistachio Cupcakes

Chocolate Pistachio Cupcakes:
1 box devil's food cake mix
1 3.4-oz. box pistachio-flavored instant pudding mix
4 eggs
⅓ C. oil
¾ C. buttermilk
½ C. sour cream
1 tsp. almond extract

Chocolate Buttercream:
1 C. butter, softened
¾ C. unsweetened cocoa powder
2 tsp. vanilla extract
3–4 C. powdered sugar
1 T. milk, if needed
Crushed pistachio nuts for decoration

Directions:

1. Preheat oven to 350 and line pans with cupcake liners.
2. Sift cake mix and pudding mix into a small bowl; set aside.
3. In a large bowl, combine eggs, oil, buttermilk, sour cream, and almond extract.
4. Add cake mix mixture and stir until smooth.
5. Fill cupcake liners ¾ full and bake for 17–22 minutes or until a knife inserted near the center comes out clean.
6. For Chocolate Buttercream: Beat butter for 1 minute. Add cocoa powder and vanilla extract and beat again. Slowly add powdered sugar until buttercream reaches desired consistency. Add 1 T. milk if the buttercream becomes too thick.
7. Pipe buttercream onto cooled cupcakes and generously top with crushed pistachios.

Makes 24 cupcakes.

Caramel Apple Cupcakes

Apple Cupcakes:
1 box white cake mix
2 tsp. cinnamon or apple pie spice
3 eggs
¼ C. butter, melted and cooled
¼ C. applesauce
1 C. milk
1 tsp. vanilla extract
1½ C. peeled, chopped apple

Caramel Buttercream:
1 C. butter, softened
2 T. caramel sauce
1 tsp. vanilla extract
3–4 C. powdered sugar
Melted caramels for drizzling

Directions:

1. Preheat oven to 350 and line pans with cupcake liners.
2. Sift cake mix and cinnamon into a small bowl; set aside.
3. In a large bowl, combine eggs, melted butter, applesauce, milk, and vanilla extract.
4. Stir in cake mix until smooth.
5. Stir in chopped apples.
6. Fill cupcake liners ¾ full and bake for 17–22 minutes or until a knife inserted near the center comes out clean.
7. For Caramel Buttercream: Beat butter for 1 minute. Add caramel and vanilla extract and continue to beat. Slowly add powdered sugar until buttercream reaches the desired consistency.
8. Pipe buttercream onto cooled cupcakes; top with melted caramel.

Makes 24 cupcakes.

yellow

Mustache Cupcakes (Father's Day)

Chocolate Cupcakes:
1 box devil's food cake mix
1 tsp. cinnamon, optional
3 eggs
½ C. butter, melted and cooled
¾ C. buttermilk or milk
¾ C. sour cream
2 tsp. vanilla extract

Cream Cheese Buttercream:
½ C. butter, softened
8 oz. cream cheese, softened
2 tsp. vanilla extract
4–5 C. powdered sugar
1 T. milk, if needed
Mustaches made with chocolate molds, out of paper, or by piping melted chocolate onto waxed paper and letting it cool

Directions:

1. Preheat oven to 350 and line pans with cupcake liners.
2. Sift cake mix and cinnamon into a small bowl; set aside.
3. In a large bowl, combine eggs, melted butter, buttermilk, sour cream, and vanilla extract.
4. Stir in cake mix/cinnamon mixture until smooth.
5. Fill cupcake liners ¾ full and bake for 17–22 minutes or until a knife inserted near the center comes out clean.
6. For Cream Cheese Buttercream: Beat butter and cream cheese for 2 minutes. Add vanilla extract. Slowly add powdered sugar until buttercream reaches desired consistency. If the buttercream becomes too thick, add milk.
7. Pipe buttercream onto cooled cupcakes and top with a stylish mustache. If you use paper mustaches, wait until just before serving to place them on the cupcakes.

Makes 24 cupcakes.

Chocolate Nest Cupcakes

Cupcakes:
1 box white cake mix
3 eggs
⅓ C. butter, melted and cooled
1 C. buttermilk
1 tsp. almond extract, optional
1 tsp. vanilla extract

Chocolate Buttercream:
1 C. butter, softened
1 tsp. vanilla extract
1 tsp. almond extract, optional
1 T. milk
½ C. unsweetened cocoa powder
3–4 C. powdered sugar
Egg-shaped candies (such as Jordan almonds) for decoration

Directions:

1. Preheat oven to 350 and line pans with cupcake liners.
2. Sift cake mix into a small bowl; set aside.
3. In a large bowl, combine eggs, melted butter, buttermilk, almond extract, and vanilla extract.
4. Stir in cake mix until smooth.
5. Fill cupcake liners ¾ full and bake for 17–22 minutes or until a knife inserted near the center comes out clean.
6. For Chocolate Buttercream: Beat butter for 1 minute. Add vanilla extract, almond extract, milk, and cocoa powder. Slowly add powdered sugar until buttercream reaches desired consistency.
7. Pipe a simple circle or a rose onto the cooled cupcakes; nestle a few egg-shaped candies in the center.

Makes 24 cupcakes.

Cakes for Kids

Most children pick a cupcake by the color of the frosting or the sprinkles on top—and they always seem to eat it from the top down. I've never seen anyone younger than ten actually make it to the cake part of a cupcake. Little kids just sit there and lick the frosting, letting it melt on their tongue. And don't try engaging them in any conversation while it happens—they're completely lost in the land of sweets.

Rainbow Cupcakes

Rainbow Cupcakes:
1 box white cake mix
4 egg whites
⅓ C. oil
1 C. milk
⅓ C. sour cream
2 tsp. vanilla extract
Red, orange, yellow, green, and blue food dye

Cloud Frosting:
1 C. butter, softened
4–6 C. powdered sugar
2 T. milk
2 tsp. vanilla extract
Gold coins for garnish

Note: Use Ateco #805 tip.

Directions:

1. Preheat oven to 350 and line pans with cupcake liners.
2. Sift cake mix into a small bowl; set aside.
3. In a large bowl, combine egg whites, oil, milk, sour cream, and vanilla extract.
4. Add cake mix and stir until well combined.
5. Divide batter evenly into 5 small bowls.
6. Add a different color of food dye to the batter in each bowl, adding a little at a time until batter is the desired shade. Stir well.
7. Fill cupcakes liners ¾ full. To achieve a layered look, put each colored batter into a small plastic bag (such as a sandwich bag); snip a bit off the corner and use the plastic bag like a mini piping bag. Beginning with the red batter, pipe a thin layer into the bottom of each cupcake liner. Pipe the next colored batter directly on top of the red batter; repeat until all colors have been used.
8. Bake for 18–22 minutes or until a knife inserted in the center comes out clean.
9. For Cloud Frosting: Beat butter for 2 minutes. Scrape down the bowl and beat for 1 more minute. Slowly add 3 C. powdered sugar. Add vanilla and milk. Continue to slowly add powdered sugar until frosting is the desired consistency.
10. Pipe frosting onto cooled cupcakes using a round tip; pipe little swirls or dots to achieve a cloudlike look. Top with a gold coin and check for leprechauns!

Makes 24 cupcakes.

Chocolate Sprinkle Cupcakes

Chocolate Cupcakes:
1 box chocolate cake mix
3 eggs
½ C. oil
¾ C. milk
¾ C. sour cream
2 tsp. vanilla extract

Vanilla Buttercream:
1 C. butter, softened
2 tsp. vanilla extract
4–5 C. powdered sugar
Milk, if needed
Multicolored sprinkles for garnish

Directions:

1. Preheat oven to 350 and line pans with cupcake liners.
2. Sift cake mix into a small bowl; set aside.
3. In a large bowl, combine eggs, oil, milk, sour cream, and vanilla extract.
4. Add cake mix and stir until smooth.
5. Fill cupcake liners ¾ full and bake for 15–20 minutes or until a knife inserted in the center comes out clean.
6. For Vanilla Buttercream: Beat butter for 2 minutes, scrape down the bowl, and beat again. Add vanilla extract. Slowly add powdered sugar until buttercream is the desired consistency.
7. Pipe onto cooled cupcakes and top with multicolored sprinkles.

Makes 24 cupcakes.

Pretty in Pink Cupcakes

Pink Confetti Cupcakes:
1 box white cake mix
4 egg whites
⅓ C. oil
¾ C. buttermilk
¾ C. sour cream
2 tsp. vanilla extract
½ tsp. almond extract (optional)
⅓ C. pink sprinkles

Strawberry Buttercream:
1 C. butter, softened
3 T. strawberry puree (process strawberries in blender)
1 tsp. vanilla extract
1 T. strawberry-flavored gelatin
4–5 C. powdered sugar
Pink sprinkles for garnish

Directions:

1. Preheat oven to 350 and line pans with cupcake liners.
2. Sift cake mix into a small bowl; set aside.
3. In a large bowl, use a whisk to gently combine egg whites, oil, buttermilk, sour cream, vanilla extract, and almond extract until smooth.
4. Add cake mix and stir.
5. Fold in pink sprinkles.
6. Fill cupcake liners ¾ full and bake for 15–20 minutes or until a knife inserted near the center comes out clean. Cool completely.
7. For Strawberry Buttercream: Beat butter for 2 minutes, scrape down the bowl, and beat again. Add strawberry puree, vanilla extract, and strawberry gelatin. Slowly add powdered sugar until buttercream is the desired consistency. Add more gelatin if desired for more color or flavor.
8. Pipe buttercream onto cooled cupcakes and top with more pink sprinkles.

Makes 24 cupcakes.

Peanut Butter Cereal Cupcakes

Chocolate Cupcakes:
1 box devil's food cake mix
3 eggs
½ C. butter, melted and cooled
1 C. buttermilk
½ C. sour cream
2 tsp. vanilla extract

Chocolate Peanut Butter Fudge Topping:
⅔ C. milk chocolate chips
⅓ C. smooth peanut butter

Peanut Butter Frosting:
¾ C. butter, softened
⅓ C. smooth peanut butter
2 tsp. vanilla extract
4–5 C. powdered sugar
2–3 T. milk
1–2 C. peanut butter cereal pieces for decoration

Directions:

1. Preheat oven to 350 and line pans with cupcake liners.
2. Sift cake mix into a small bowl; set aside.
3. In a large bowl, use a whisk to gently combine eggs, melted butter (make sure it's cool), buttermilk, sour cream, and vanilla extract.
4. Add cake mix and stir until smooth.
5. Fill cupcake liners ¾ full and bake for 15–20 minutes or until a knife inserted near the center comes out clean. Cool completely.
6. For Chocolate Peanut Butter Fudge Topping: In a small pan, combine chocolate chips and peanut butter; melt over medium heat and constantly stir until smooth. Let cool slightly then dip the tops of cooled cupcakes into the chocolate. If the chocolate drips down the liner, let the chocolate cool a little longer.
7. For Peanut Butter Frosting: Beat butter and peanut butter until smooth. Add vanilla extract and slowly add powdered sugar. Stream in a little bit of milk at a time until frosting is the desired consistency. Use more powdered sugar to thicken if needed.
8. Let the fudge topping on the cupcakes become firm, then pipe a small mound of frosting over it.
9. Press the cereal pieces into the cake—or let the kids do it when they get home from school.

Makes 24 cupcakes.

puffs

Chocolate Chip Cupcakes

Chocolate Chip Cupcakes:
1 box white cake mix
3 eggs
⅓ C. butter, melted and cooled
¾ C. milk
¾ C. sour cream
1 T. vanilla extract
1 C. mini chocolate chips

Chocolate Buttercream:
1 C. butter, softened
¾ C. unsweetened cocoa powder
2 tsp. vanilla extract
1 T. milk
3–4 C. powdered sugar
Mini chocolate chips for garnish

Directions:

1. Preheat oven to 350 and line pans with cupcake liners.
2. Sift cake mix into a small bowl; set aside.
3. In a large bowl, use a whisk to gently combine eggs, melted butter (make sure it's cooled), milk, sour cream, and vanilla extract.
4. Add cake mix and stir until smooth.
5. Stir in mini chocolate chips.
6. Fill cupcake liners ¾ full and bake for 15–20 minutes or until a knife inserted near the center comes out clean.
7. For Chocolate Buttercream: Beat butter for 2 minutes, scrape down the bowl, and beat again. Add cocoa, vanilla extract, and milk. Slowly add powdered sugar until buttercream reaches desired consistency. Add more milk if the buttercream becomes too thick.
8. Pipe buttercream onto cooled cupcakes and top with extra mini chocolate chips.

Makes 24 cupcakes.

Peanut Butter and Jelly Cupcakes

Peanut Butter Cupcakes:
1 box white cake mix
½ C. smooth peanut butter
½ C. butter, softened
3 eggs
⅔ C. milk
½ C. sour cream
2 tsp. vanilla extract

Peanut Butter Fudge Topping:
⅓ C. smooth peanut butter
⅔ C. white chocolate chips

Strawberry Jelly Frosting:
1 C. butter, softened
¼ C. strawberry jelly or jam
1 T. strawberry-flavored gelatin
1 tsp. vanilla extract
4–5 C. powdered sugar
Extra jelly or jam for garnish

Directions:

1. Preheat oven to 350 and line pans with cupcake liners.
2. Sift cake mix into a small bowl; set aside.
3. With a stand mixer, beat ½ C. peanut butter and ½ C. butter until smooth. Scrape down the sides of the bowl and beat again.
4. With the mixer on slow, add eggs one at a time and beat until incorporated. Add milk, sour cream, and vanilla extract.
5. Add cake mix and mix until smooth.
6. Fill cupcake liners ¾ full and bake for 15–20 minutes or until a knife inserted near the center comes out clean. Cool completely.
7. For Peanut Butter Fudge Topping: Melt ⅓ C. peanut butter and white chocolate chips over low heat. Stir constantly until smooth. White chocolate can burn easily, so be careful. Remove from heat and let it cool for a few minutes.
8. Dip the top of cooled cupcakes into the peanut butter fudge topping. If the fudge drips onto the cupcake liner, let the peanut butter fudge cool a little longer. Let the fudge become firm before frosting.
9. For Strawberry Jelly Frosting: Beat butter for 2 minutes. Add jelly, gelatin, and vanilla extract; beat. Scrape down the sides of the bowl and slowly add powdered sugar until frosting reaches desired consistency. Add more gelatin if desired for more color or strawberry taste.
10. Pipe frosting over the peanut butter fudge topping; top with a little bit of strawberry jelly. Top with additional jelly or jam.

Note: If you use jam, do not try to pipe the frosting with a star tip. The seeds in the jam may clog the piping tip. Either strain out the seeds or use a circle piping tip.

Makes 24 cupcakes.

Snow Cone Cupcakes

Vanilla Cupcakes:
1 box white cake mix
4 egg whites
⅓ C. oil
¾ C. milk
¾ C. sour cream
2 tsp. vanilla extract

Frosting:
1½ C. butter, softened
5–7 C. powdered sugar
2–3 T. milk
1–2 T. lemon-flavored gelatin
1–2 T. cherry-flavored gelatin
1–2 T. blue berry-flavored gelatin
Coarse sugar sprinkles in yellow, red, and blue for garnish

Directions:

1. Preheat oven to 350 and line pans with cupcake liners; you can also use soufflé cups.
2. Sift cake mix into a small bowl; set aside.
3. In a large bowl, use a whisk to gently combine egg whites, oil, milk, sour cream, and vanilla extract.
4. Add cake mix and stir until smooth.
5. Fill cupcake liners ¾ full and bake for 15–20 minutes or until a knife inserted near the center comes out clean.
6. For Frosting: Beat butter for 2 minutes; scrape down the sides of the bowl. Gradually add powdered sugar until frosting is the desired consistency. Add a little milk if it becomes too thick.
7. Divide frosting evenly into three small bowls. Add a different flavored gelatin to the frosting in each bowl; mix well. Taste and add more gelatin if needed.
8. To assemble, pipe a stripe of yellow frosting across each cupcake. Use a knife to smooth it out into a sort of Mohawk on the cupcake. Roll the top of the yellow stripe into the yellow sprinkles.
9. Pipe red frosting on either side of the yellow stripe. Use a knife to smooth out the frosting and fill in the needed areas. Roll the red frosting into a small bowl of red sprinkles. (The red sprinkles will not stick to the yellow area if the yellow area is fully covered in yellow sprinkles.)
10. Repeat using the blue frosting and blue sprinkles.
11. Once the cupcake is completely covered in sprinkles, use your clean hand to round out the top of the cupcake and to smooth the edges between each flavored stripe.

Makes 24 cupcakes.

Tips and Tricks

"What bakery did you get these from?" That's one of my favorite questions. Whenever I bake a batch of cupcakes, I want them to taste and look like they came from the best bakery in town. I want them to be decked out with fluffy frosting, dipped in rich ganache, and topped with something spectacular.

How to Make Basic Buttercream

Start with butter at room temperature; it should be soft to the touch. Never soften or melt butter in the microwave; even if you let it solidify again, it won't work well.

Place the butter in a stand mixer and let it beat for 2–3 minutes on medium speed.

Add flavorings, such as extracts or cocoa, and beat again.

Slowly add powdered sugar until the buttercream reaches the desired consistency.

If it becomes too thick, add a little milk to thin it out.

Avoid these common mistakes:

- Using margarine instead of butter: Using real butter gives a better taste and creates a better texture.
- Melting the butter: Just don't do it. You won't get a light, whipped texture if you do.
- Adding too much berry puree: Working with berry puree can be tricky. You want to use enough puree so that the taste comes through, but if you use too much the buttercream will start to separate or will never firm up. I recommend adding the berry puree last so you're less likely to use too much.

Piping

Choosing a Piping Tip

Choose the tip you'll use with buttercream in mind. Piping tips that have very small openings, like a Wilton 2D, look great but have a downside: The buttercream has to be perfectly smooth—if it's not, the tip will clog. If the buttercream contains strawberry seeds or cookie crumbs, a small, closed-star tip is risky.

Tip Types

1. Open star—the triangles go straight out
2. Closed star—the triangles close into the center
3. Circle—this may look like it's the most simple but it is the most difficult tip to use because it shows every flaw

How to Fill a Piping Bag

- Slide the piping tip into the bag and push it into the hole until snug. Make sure the little triangles are not covered by the bag. If any are covered, remove the piping tip and use scissors to trim the bag.
- Turn the top of the bag inside out.
- Fill the bag with buttercream or frosting using either the cup method or the hand method.

Cup Method

- Place the bag inside a tall glass or cup with the top of the bag hanging over the edge of the glass, inside out.
- Put a scoop full of frosting in the bag, using the edge of the glass to scrape off the frosting.
- Lift the bag from the glass and pull the top of the bag right side out.
- Twist the bag right above where the frosting is; continue twisting to push the frosting down the inside of the bag until it starts to come out of the tip.

Hand Method

- Turn the bag inside out.
- Make a C shape with your hand then place your hand inside the bag.
- Use the side of your hand to scrape the frosting onto and into the bag.
- Once the bag is filled, turn the bag right-side out and twist the bag right above the frosting.
- Continue twisting the bag to push the frosting down the inside of the bag until it starts to come out of the tip.

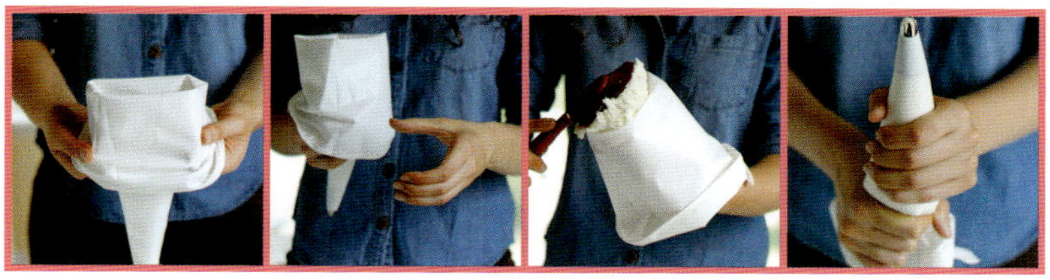

Classic Bakery Swirl

Always squeeze the piping bag from the back, away from the piping tip. If you squeeze just above the piping tip, half the frosting will go out through the tip and the other half will go out the top of the bag—and you'll have a big mess.

Using constant pressure, start at the center of the cupcake and pipe a circle around the edge of the cupcake. Continue, still using constant pressure, to pipe consecutively smaller circles on top of the first one. (I usually pipe about three circles, with each circle is smaller than the last.)

When you reach the top of the frosting spiral, release pressure from the bag and lift up.

Rose Technique

While the bakery swirl starts with a large circle that gets consecutively smaller, the rose technique does the opposite.

Starting at the center of the cupcake, pipe a spiral going out toward the edge of the cupcake. When you reach the edge, release the pressure and pull the piping bag away.

Practice by piping on the bottom of a drinking glass; most are about the same size as the surface of a cupcake. After you pipe the frosting, scrape it back into the bowl and use it again.

Ganache

In a microwave-safe bowl, combine chocolate chips and whipping cream.
Heat in the microwave for about 20–40 seconds, or until the chocolate begins to melt.
Using a spoon or a small whisk, stir the chocolate until smooth.
Dip the cupcake into the ganache.
Let the ganache cool completely until set.

Tip: I like to dip just one cupcake first to make sure the ganache doesn't drip down the sides. If it does drip, wait for the ganache to cool a little before dipping the rest.

If you have extra ganache, put it in a plastic container and refrigerate it. It will be good for a few days. When you bake again, you can heat it up in the microwave and use it again!

Frequently Asked Questions

Q: What adjustment should I make if I'm at a high altitude?
A: At high altitudes, cupcakes rise too fast. As a result, they can overflow in the oven and always have flat tops. To compensate, fill your cupcake liners less than normal.

Q: What's the best way to store cupcakes?
A: Cupcakes should be stored in airtight containers. I always try to bake my cupcakes the day I'll be serving them, but if I'm baking for a large event, I bake the cakes the night before and store them in airtight containers. Then I make the buttercreams and fillings the day of the event and assemble them that day. If you refrigerate buttercream, it will turn rock hard, so make sure you remove it from the refrigerator with plenty of time for it to reach room temperature.

Q: Should I refrigerate or freeze cupcakes?
A: Always freeze them—refrigeration will dry out your cupcakes.

Q: What's the best piping tip for a beginner?
A: A closed-star tip. It looks fancy and professional but it covers up any flaws a beginner might make.

Q: What's the best way to transport cupcakes?
A: I always try to pipe my cupcakes where they will be served. I transport the cupcakes in large plastic food containers and transport any frostings or garnishes in big tubs. If I'm transporting just a small number of cupcakes, I use bakery boxes. You can buy them at restaurant supply stores or online.

Q: Why do you use sour cream so much in your recipes?
A: Cake mixes tend to be very light; sour cream helps give them extra body and richness. It also keeps them very moist.

Q: What type of cupcake liners do you use?
A: I almost always use greaseproof liners. They tend to be a little thicker than normal liners and are a little more expensive but they keep their color and decoration after baking. Keep in mind that baking a chocolate cupcake in a liner and baking a vanilla cupcake in a liner will not

yield the same look. Also, there's a wide range of quality even among greaseproof liners. The first time I buy a specific brand of liner, I buy just a small amount; if I like them after I bake in them, I buy in bulk.

Q: How do you get all your cupcakes the same size?

A: I use what's called a food scoop. Remember when the lunch lady in the cafeteria scooped up your serving of lunch-surprise and it would be in a perfect round portion? She was using a food scoop! They are usually available at regular stores, but you can always find them at restaurant supply stores and online. They're a great tool because they take less time to fill your liners—and they're great for cookies too!

Q: How do I know if my cupcakes are done?

A: Insert a sharp knife into the center of a cupcake. If the knife comes out with wet batter on it, then the cupcake isn't done. If the knife comes out clean or has just a few normal cake crumbs on it, then the cupcakes are done! You can also simply press the top of the cupcake lightly with your finger. If the cupcake springs back, the cupcakes are done. If an indentation from your finger stays on the cupcake, leave them in the oven for a few more minutes.

Q: Can I use your recipes for a cake instead of cupcakes?

A: Yes, you can! The baking time will be a little bit longer, so check the doneness using a toothpick or knife inserted into the center of the cake.

Q: Do you do all your own photography?

A: Yes, I do. But until I get a third hand (or a husband), I sometimes have to beg a roommate or friend to take a photo of me doing a process shot.

Q: What's the most important thing about food photography?

A: Natural light. Set up a little table by a window in your house and do your photos there. You can also set up outside or on the patio in the shade. Whether you're inside or outdoors, direct light is too harsh.

Index

C

D

E

F

G

H

I

J

L

S

T

V

W

Y

Z